Praise for *When All the Stars Align*

"Les Goldberg's *When All the Stars Align* feels like a book that was delivered from the heavens to be life's handbook for both business and life. What an inspiring read and workbook."

David Adler
CEO and Founder, BizBash Media

"*When All the Stars Align* offers helpful and relevant insight into the mindset, strategy, and attitude that has helped Les not only build a great business but find personal contentment as well. Having founded and grown a business myself, I agree with absolutely everything he writes and find much of it at play in my own journey."

Justin Wetherill
CEO and Co-founder, uBreakiFix

"When does your life need improvement? It always does. *When All the Stars Align* is a brilliant roadmap for anyone and everyone looking for the path to a successful life. Les covers all of the essential elements for personal and business success, including helping others to achieve their own successes."

Martin A. Rubin
President and CEO, Smart City Holdings

"*When All the Stars Align* is a rich insightful offering from a business leader who has come of age. Especially suitable for younger readers looking to chart a course towards a successful and meaningful life."

Huntly Christie
Entrepreneur

"Les has written a generous, encouraging, and inspirational book which teaches us two valuable lessons: First, that unless we are totally committed to doing the hard work, our personal relationships will only provide us supportive benefits. Second, and more importantly, our success is of our own doing and the alignment of our stars is controlled from within."

Dr. T̶̶̶ ̶̶̶

Entertainment exec̶̶̶̶

D1413952

WHEN ALL

THE

STARS ALIGN

WHEN ALL

THE

STARS ALIGN

Create a Life Where Great Things Happen

LES M. GOLDBERG

Cover design: Jerry D. Clement
Interior design & production: Tuscawilla Creative Services

Courage to Dream Media
2350 Investors Row
Orlando, FL 32837

This publication is designed to provide accurate and authoritative information in regard to the subject matter covered. It is sold with the understanding that the publisher and author are not engaged in rendering legal, accounting or other professional services. If legal advice or other expert assistance is required, the services of a competent professional person should be sought.

When All the Stars Align: Create a Life Where Great Things Happen / Les M. Goldberg

ISBN 978-0-9963548-2-0

For my beautiful wife, Julie,
and our three incredible children,
Sydney, Lindsey, and Hunter,
who have been a part of my journey
since before they were born.

CONTENTS

CHAPTER ONE

WINNING THE LOTTERY

What would it mean to you if you won the lottery?

We've all seen the commercials for Publisher's Clearing House where they run up and surprise someone with a huge check and the promise of regular payments for life. We've read the news reports about people who win millions of dollars in various lotteries. And we've heard stories of people who inherit large sums of money or get a huge award in a lawsuit.

What would receiving that kind of cash windfall mean to you? What would change in your life? What would you do?

I feel like I won the lottery a long time ago and just didn't realize it at the time.

Winning the lottery is about more than just a big check. It's about more than money. It's about the freedom to do what you want, when you want, and how you want. It's about using your life in the best possible way because you're not limited by a lack of resources. It's about pursuing your dreams with nothing to hold you back.

And you know what? You can win the lottery without ever buying a ticket. I know because I did.

I work in a world I enjoy where I get to build and create and conquer with people I care about. So many people are *not* fortunate enough to love what they do, enjoy the people they work with, be passionate about whatever it is they produce, and know they are making a difference. I'm in that place, and I know how blessed I am. If I won millions of dollars in the lottery today, there's nothing about my life that I would change.

I didn't get here by chance. I realize that to an outsider, it might look like I got lucky as I was starting and growing my business. It's true that many times along the way, things beyond my control happened that worked to my benefit. Of course, there were plenty of times that things beyond my control worked to my detriment and I had to deal with it. But regardless of what was happening, I was an active participant. I didn't sit back and let life flow around me.

It's possible for each of us to make our own stars align, to make things great things happen on a regular and consistent basis.

The title and theme of this book come from a phrase that commonly means things have come together just right in your life. Many people think that when your stars align, it's due to pure luck or maybe divine intervention— it's like winning the lottery. I disagree. I think it's possible for each of us to make our stars align, to make great things happen on a regular and consistent basis.

As I look back on my life, I realize that yes, my stars had aligned. But not by accident. And I want to show you how you can apply the same philosophies and strategies I did to take control of your life and career to create circumstances that will not only allow you to achieve success, however you define it, but let you wake up every morning knowing that your stars are aligned and feeling like you've won the lottery.

Even though the message of this book is strongly focused on work and career, that's not all there is in life. We all have—or should have—a personal life that includes family, friends, social activities, non-work interests, and so on. It's impossible to put a price on the value of that, but when I look at my family, I feel like I won the lottery there, too. Keep that in mind as you read. Think about how you can apply the strategies and tactics that will help your professional stars align in your personal life as well.

At the end of each chapter is a section called Homework. It's a word I use when I'm making sure people know what they need to do. For example, if we've had a meeting to discuss putting together a bid on a project, at the end of it, I might say, "So, Bob, your homework is to get the equipment costs and Mary, your homework is to map out the logistics." I don't mean literal homework (although sometimes we do take work home with us); I mean, this is what you need to do next so we can achieve our goals.

I encourage you to take the homework assignments seriously. They're what puts the message of this book on steroids.

I hope this book inspires you to think about where you are in life and where you want to be, to celebrate your accomplishments, and to figure out what you need to do to make all of your stars align.

Homework

List the top three things that would change in your life if you received a significant financial windfall.

_____

_____

_____

_____

_____

_____

Can you make any portion of those changes without the money? Which one(s) and how?

_____

_____

_____

_____

_____

_____

CHAPTER TWO

DREAMS, DRIVE & DIRECTION

You've heard people talk about situations when all the stars aligned. They meant that all the pieces fell into place, all the moving parts of a project were perfectly synchronized, and all of the people knew what they had to do, had the necessary and appropriate skills and tools to do it, and executed flawlessly. The result was success.

Did that happen by accident? By coincidence? Was it fate or luck?

No. Not even close.

The stars fall into alignment for people who put themselves in a position to achieve success. Who know what they want. Who show up at the right place at the right time, pay attention, and do the hard work.

The success (some people call it luck and we'll talk

more about that in Chapter 6) that comes when the stars align begins with dreams, drive, and direction.

I'm not talking about the dreams you have when you're sleeping. I'm talking about the dreams you have when you're wide awake—those aspirational dreams and desires that may seem crazy and far-fetched, but when you break them down into goals and develop a plan, you realize they're achievable. Those dreams are the building blocks of your life, the foundation that is essential for the stars to align in your world.

While dreams are important, they're not enough. Turning your dreams into reality also requires drive and direction.

Drive is about how bad you want it, how hard you're willing to work to earn it or achieve it. Drive is about *Connect your dreams to goals to create the action that will produce results.* not giving up, about persevering and overcoming obstacles that might cause others to quit. Drive is about how much fuel is in your tank and how you refuel when your tank is low.

Direction is about knowing where you want to go and how you're going to get there. It's the understanding that if you don't know where you're going, you won't know if you ever get there. It's being honest with yourself about where you're going. With direction, you can focus your energy and efforts. When you have to make choices, having direction helps you avoid making poor choices.

Dreams, drive, and direction working together are essential for making the stars align. When I was young and just getting started in my business, I knew this intuitively.

I did it instinctively. As I matured and grew my company, I understood it better and learned how to be purposeful about it. You can do the same.

Put your dreams on the road to reality

Dreams never just magically come true. Life is challenging. Good things are rarely just handed to us. Accomplishing great things is not easy. But if you set goals then develop and implement a plan, it's possible to turn your dreams into reality.

Dreams begin in your imagination. You need them to move forward. But by themselves, dreams don't mean much, and they don't *do* anything. Connecting your dreams to goals will create the actions that can produce results.

How do you start moving your dreams from fantasy to reality? First, write them down. All of them. Don't try to edit or judge them as you write—just get them on paper so you can see them. You can't know if your stars have aligned if you don't know what it will look like when they do.

Maybe your dream is to have a particular career or to own a business. Maybe it's to be a professional athlete or an Olympic gold medalist. Or to travel and enjoy luxury vacations or to live in a certain place or a particular style of house. Maybe you dream about having certain relationships in your life—a spouse, friends, children, other family—or being wealthy and famous. No matter how unrealistic your dreams may seem, you should acknowledge them and write them down. You don't have to tell anyone else about them. It's okay to keep them private but writing them down will clarify them for you and give you an important starting point.

The next step is to determine which ones you are most passionate about and are possible—not necessarily probable, but possible. For example, you may have a dream of being an astronaut, but if you're in your 50s with none of the prerequisite experience or training, it's not likely to happen. You may have a dream of being a professional athlete, but if you don't have the necessary physical attributes—height for basketball players, balance and flexibility for gymnasts, hand-eye coordination for tennis players, etc.—you're probably going to maintain an amateur status. When you were a child, you might have dreamed of being a superhero or a Disney princess. Those dreams are not possible. But you might have a dream of a new career or starting a business—that's possible at virtually any age. You might have a dream of achieving a certain degree of financial wealth—again, that's possible.

Once you cross off the impossible dreams, take a look at what's left. For each one, determine what it would take to turn the dream into reality. What does it require in terms of conditions and resources such as time, money, and effort? This process should take some research, but it's something you have to know before you can decide if you're willing and able to invest the time, spend the money, and make the effort to get the results you want.

Olympic athletes are a perfect example of this. Of the 7.6 billion people on the planet today, how many of them are gymnasts? I don't know, but I'd say easily millions, especially if you consider all the kids who take gymnastics when they're little. How many of them ever get to compete at the Olympics? Very few. That's because getting to the Olympics takes more than talent and skill—it takes motivation, drive, discipline, and sacrifice. It also takes resources including time, money, access to coaches and training facilities, and more. I'm sure there are plenty of gymnasts who have the ability to perform at the Olympic level but they don't, either because they don't have the resources or they aren't willing to do what it takes.

My point is not to fault the gymnasts who decide they don't want to make the sacrifices necessary to reach the elite level in their sport. There's nothing wrong with deciding you don't want to train six to eight hours a day and do the other things required for professional sports

The saying "you get what you pay for" is never truer than when applied to the concept of effort expended for results received.

success. But if you don't know what it will take to turn a dream into reality, you'll never be able to do it, whether you want to or not.

The idea here is not to burst bubbles and kill dreams—it's to help you turn your most passionate dreams into steps and goals. It's to help you figure out what you have to do to get your dreams out of your imagination and into your real life. Too many people spend too much time and money going to school studying things that have nothing to do with their dreams. They pursue opportunities that involve things they don't like doing. Or they find themselves on a path to a place they don't want to go and they can't figure out why they're going that way. They feel like their stars never align—and they're right. Don't be one of those people. Find that balance between being realistic and pursuing your dreams that will point you in the right direction for your life's journey.

Once you've figured out which of your dreams are actually possible and what you have to do to achieve them, you need to prioritize them and make a plan. Your plan needs to include goals—not just the primary goal of your dream, but incremental goals that you can use to measure your progress. There's a saying you can always apply when you're working on your objectives: The best way to eat an elephant (primary goal) is one bite at a time (incremental goals).

I'm not going to take a lot of time talking about goal-setting. You can find plenty of other resources to

S.M.A.R.T. Goals

Specific. Clearly and concisely define what you're going to do.

Measurable. Be able to track your progress. Know what tangible evidence will demonstrate that you've accomplished the goal. Measure outcomes, not activities.

Achievable. Though your goal should be challenging and force you to stretch to reach it, it must also be attainable. Be sure you have or can get the knowledge, skills, and resources necessary to accomplish the goal.

Relevant. Your goal should relate to your overall life plan. Don't bother setting goals that don't really mean anything to you.

Timely. Create a schedule for achieving the goal. Give yourself a deadline and commit to meeting it.

help you with that. Do an Amazon book search on "how to set goals" and you'll get more than 500 results—that's 500 books that will tell you how to set goals. That same search on Google generates more than 600 million results for articles, videos, books and more on setting goals. Just remember that you don't need to make goal-setting complicated. Set what's commonly known as S.M.A.R.T. goals—goals that are specific, measurable, achievable, relevant, and timely.

Motivation: What drives you toward your dreams?

Drive is something that exists within us. We all have it— it's like a jet engine inside of us. Is your jet engine idling in the hangar, growling on the taxiway, or roaring into the sky? If your jet engine is going to roar, it has to be about something you're totally committed to. When you have a clearly defined dream that's connected to your passion, you can turn on your drive. Driven people achieve more because they have something that's pushing them forward, that's motivating them to succeed.

What is motivation? It's what drives us. And it's different for all of us. If you're going to make your stars align, you have to figure out what motivates you. Doing this takes some serious introspection and soul-searching. You need to understand what you want—that is, what you yourself truly want, not what someone else might want for you—and how hard you're willing to work to get it. Some people are motivated by monetary rewards. Some are motivated by recognition and public praise. Some are motivated by personal satisfaction. And the list goes on.

The strength of your motivation has a direct bearing on how hard you're willing to work. For example, let's say I'm hungry and I'm in the mood for a gourmet meal. It doesn't take a lot of motivation for me to go into a five-star restaurant and order my favorite dishes that someone else cooks. That's easy—I just get in my car and go. But cooking that gourmet meal at home means I have to plan a menu, go to the store, buy the ingredients, come home, prepare them, eat, and then clean up. That takes a lot more motivation—and effort—than going to a restaurant.

If I want to create something excellent, it's going to take work. I have to put in the time and energy to acquire the necessary knowledge and skills—and then more time and energy to do the work. But I believe that anything worth having is worth working for. The saying "you get what you pay for" is never truer than when applied to the concept of effort expended for results received. If you're not motivated to work hard, you're not likely to see much in the way of results.

Motivation is what makes it possible for us to reach deep inside ourselves and say, "I can do that," whether it's running a marathon, climbing a mountain, or tackling a business challenge. When I want to achieve something and I have a goal, I am extremely motivated.

Appreciate the unknown

We don't know the future. We can plan, we can prepare, we can do our best to make things turn out the way we want—and often they will. But sometimes they won't. Sometimes there's a bump in the road, sometimes there's a mountain in our way, and we have to be able to either change course or work through it. But if we know our-selves, if we have clear goals and understand what drives us, we can deal with all those surprises life puts in our way.

I think not knowing the future is what makes it so exciting. With any endeavor, we believe we'll succeed, but we know we could fail—and win or lose, we're going to have unique experiences.

The Cleveland Cavaliers are a great example of this kind of optimism. On a Friday in 2016, we received a call from the team saying they were planning a parade in downtown Cleveland for the following week because they were going to win the NBA championship. Of course, they didn't know for sure, but they had confidence in their team. We agreed to send trucks of equipment—three from Orlando, one from Baltimore, one from Detroit—and be

Embrace the possibilities

Keep a positive and open mind as you embrace the possibilities of your dreams. Think in big, bold terms. What would it be like to have a helicopter so you could avoid city traffic? It's possible if you have enough money. What would it be like to be a doctor? It's possible if you can make the commitment to go to school, earn the neces-sary degree, and get the post-graduate training.

When people close their minds, when they don't give themselves the chance to dream, when they reject their dreams as impossible—that's when they fail. Sadly, not many people can say "yes" when asked if they have their dream job and if they're living their dreams. Be that person! Embrace the possibilities and start living your dream right now.

ready to stage the parade in Cleveland. The deal was that they would pay us a large sum of money if they won the championship and the parade took place. But if they lost and didn't have the parade, they would pay us a nominal sum to cover our costs of prepping the gear, transporting it to Cleveland, and having it out of service for that period of time.

If you're a basketball fan, you know that the Cavaliers won the title in the final minute of game seven on Sunday. Both of our teams won—the Cavaliers on the basketball court and our team by being in place to help them celebrate.

The Italian poet Dante wrote, "If you can see the road ahead, it is not worth the trip." The future is the ultimate unknown—and too many people fear the unknown. Successful people don't. Instead, they embrace the unknown with open arms. They see it as an adventure. As I said, they plan. They prepare. They calculate probabilities and possibilities. They create contingencies. And then they move ahead and enjoy the ride.

Here's one final point on this topic that I want to stress: While you don't know the future, it's important to know yourself. Know who you are, what you want, what's going to make you happy so you don't waste time floundering in a fantasy land. Knowing who you are will help you connect your drive to your dream.

Know where you're going

I meet a lot of people who lack direction. They may have a dream, they may have drive and motivation, but they don't know which way to go. More of them tend to be younger, in the under 30 generation, but I know some older ones as well. These are people who haven't figured out what they want to do, where they want to go, how they want to live. They're just drifting without any real control over their lives. Their stars will not align until they have a direction.

People have told me that I'm special because I knew what I wanted to do at a young age. It's true that I discovered the business I wanted to be in while I was in high school, but not before I experimented with other ventures, including lawn mowing, marketing, buying and selling merchandise at flea markets and other venues, videography, and even a brief stint in a fast

The earlier we discover our direction, the easier it is to map a life journey where the stars are aligned.

food restaurant. I share the details of these efforts in my book *Don't Take No for an Answer*. But it wasn't figuring out my direction that was special, it was that as a teenager I managed to get exposure to a range of careers and industries so that I could figure out what I liked and didn't like. I don't think many young people today are getting that kind of experience.

In my opinion, every high school should offer a required class that will give kids a real-world view of a variety of career paths so they can begin determining their direction. Along with administering career aptitude tests, these classes should bring in people who can speak to what it's like to work in a wide range of occupations. And parents need to be involved as well. Don't just hope your kids will determine their path in life—help them as best you can. Show them what you do and ask your friends to share details of their careers with your kids as well. Don't try to decide *for* your kids, but help them figure out for themselves what they would like to do, what they will be good at doing, and then how they can turn that knowledge into a rewarding career or business.

Experience helps us define our dreams and develop drive—our inner passion and commitment—so we can get our lives going in the best direction. The earlier we discover our direction, the easier it is to map a life journey where the stars are aligned.

What does the finish line look like?

Whenever I start a new project, one of the first things I do is imagine the finish. I mentally begin at the end so I can back up and figure out what I need to do to get there. I do the same thing when I'm making proposals to customers— before I get down to the nitty-gritty details, I try to mentally take them to the finish, to get them to imagine the day when the event happens or the installation is complete. When you've decided to do something, visualize it completed. What will you have achieved? What does it look like? How does it feel? How will it impact your life?

Some people call this process vision. It's the ability to have an idea and know what the final product will be. A friend of mine who is a real estate developer has the amazing ability to look at raw land and know what it's going to look like when construction is finished. People like Bill Gates and Steve Jobs have that kind of vision. And you can develop it for yourself.

We have a lot of different finish lines in our lives. Some are for one-time projects that have a clear lifecycle—

completing school, getting a promotion at work, even writing a book like this one. Some are grander and may be harder to define. And the biggest one of all is, of course, that finish line that signals the end of your life. You don't want to get to that final finish line with regret. You want to get there feeling that your life has had meaning, that you have accomplished things you wanted to do, that the world is at least a little better because you were in it. If you want to get to your deathbed with no regrets, what do you have to do now?

Homework

Make a list of your dreams and cross off the obviously impossible ones.

_____

_____

_____

_____

_____

_____

_____

_____

_____

_____

_____

Rank the remaining possible dreams on your list in order of your desire to make them come true.

_____

_____

_____

_____

_____

_____

_____

_____

_____

_____

_____

Next to your number one dream, write down what will motivate you to turn it into reality.

_____

_____

_____

_____

_____

Describe the finish line of your number one dream.

_____

_____

_____

_____

_____

CHAPTER THREE

KNOW YOUR WHY

Everyone has a purpose. Some people know what their purpose is; others don't have a clue. If you want your stars to align, you must understand your purpose.

Your purpose is your why. It's your reason for being. It fuels everything you do. It gives you a sense of self-worth. It validates your existence. It's what makes you happy.

Some people have a simple and obvious purpose. They know what it is at an early age and pursue it relentlessly. Mother Teresa is a great example. She always knew her why and it guided her in everything she did. At a young age, she was called to be a missionary. She became a nun, teaching at St. Mary's School in Calcutta. More than a decade later, she received her "call within a call" to establish a religious community dedicated to serving the poorest of the poor. She was still a missionary, still serving, just doing it differently. For most of us, however, figuring out our purpose is not quite so easy. It takes a great deal of thought and introspection, usually over a period of time and often through many life lessons. A good way to begin understanding your purpose is to ask yourself, "How do I want to be remembered?"

Most purposes are multi-layered. You may feel that your purpose is to make a positive difference in the world. That's great, but it barely scratches the surface. How are you going to do it? What will it look like? Dig further to refine your purpose so you can incorporate it into your dreams, drive, and direction. You could make a positive difference by teaching, but are you going to teach first graders or medical students? You could make a positive difference by being a mentor, but are you going to mentor an at-risk youth or a professional colleague? You could make a positive difference by building a company that provides great products and services for its customers and jobs for its employees, but what kind of company should it be? Go deep through the layers of your purpose so you genuinely understand and can articulate it.

Knowing your why gives you the super-strength you need to achieve incredible goals.

In addition to being multi-layered, purposes are multi-dimensional. You can have one purpose for your career or your company, another for your home life, and even still another for community service and social issues. Even as those purposes overlap, there's a strong chance they'll have some distinct differences. It's also likely that your individual purposes and how you live them will evolve as you do. As you gain life experience and new skills, the way you manifest your purpose will change. You might, for example, go from doing a particular job to teaching others how to do it or even to developing better ways to do it. It's fair to say that Thomas Edison's purpose was to be an inventor—and he was one of the top inventors of all time. From childhood, he loved to experiment, and that's how his purpose manifested. But as he grew into adulthood and gained knowledge and experience, he was able to establish a research laboratory and entrepreneurial ventures through which his inventions were made commercially available. His fundamental purpose didn't change, but the way he lived it did. Instead of experimenting on his own, he expanded his team and made sure his discoveries were widely accessible.

Think of at least three people you admire (living or not, and you don't have to know them personally) who understood their purpose from a young age and lived it for their entire lives. What can you learn from those people? How can they serve as a model for your life?

Figure out your destiny

The most popular definition of destiny is *a pre-determined state or end*. I believe in destiny. I believe that if things are meant to be, they will happen. Where I am right now, personally and professionally, is my destiny. I was meant to do what I do as a business owner and a family man. Even though I probably could have done several other things and been successful, I couldn't have done anything else better. But that doesn't mean I didn't have to work for it—and work hard.

When you hear phrases like "destined for greatness"

or "born for this job or role," it doesn't mean those people can sit back and coast their way to success. Even the children born into royal families have to work in their positions. When you find out what you're good at and connect it to your dreams, you'll be able to figure out what you are meant to do—your destiny. But you can't achieve your destiny without effort. When people talk about destiny, they often say things like, "It was written in the stars." If something is going to be written in your stars, it will be because you write it there. It won't just happen; it will require action.

Much like your purpose, when you understand your destiny, you can figure out how to reach it.

Ask the question to get the answer

Probably the most common question children ask is "Why?" They want to know the why of everything—why is the sky blue; why do people have different skin, hair, and eye colors; why do you *love* one person, merely *like* another, and intensely *dislike* someone else? When I was a kid, I was always asking why. I drove my parents crazy. I couldn't get enough answers. Why is it so hot in the summer? Why can't we air condition the outside? Why are planes able to fly?

It works to think like a child and ask why about everything as you define your purpose. Once you know your *why*, you can get to work on the *what* and *how*. Knowing your why gives you the super-strength you need to achieve incredible goals.

Let's address the issue of money here. Though you may want to have a lot of money—and that's fine—getting financially rich is not your why. We don't exist to make money. If you study successful people, you'll see that their why is not money. Money is a byproduct of understanding and living your purpose and of being successful.

The vision and mission statements of my company say nothing about making money. Of course, we need to be profitable—that's essential if we're going to stay in business and grow—but we are not motivated solely by money. We are motivated by a desire to build relationships and deliver extraordinary experiences through technology and imagination. That we make money doing it is the icing on the cake. In a *Wall Street Journal* interview, John Mackey, CEO and founder of Whole Foods Market, Inc., said, "Most of the companies I admire in the world I think have a deeper purpose. I've met a lot of successful entrepreneurs. They all started their businesses not to maximize shareholder value but to pursue a dream."

What makes you happy?

Do you know what makes you happy?

Happiness is essential to living a life where the stars are aligned. We need to know what makes us happy, and it's easier to figure that out when we know our why. I've always said that happiness is not a destination, it's a way to travel. You don't want to wait to be happy until you arrive at a particular place or achieve a particular goal— you want to be happy every day. You want to live a happy life. Something I've more recently discovered is that sometimes the people who live the simplest lives have the highest degree of happiness.

I recognize that we live in a complex world, but it still

doesn't have to take a lot to make someone happy. Things don't have to be complicated to make us happy. All too often, we don't celebrate the little things of happiness— things as simple as ice cream and sunsets. We should be happy for refrigeration and air conditioning, for living in an age of airplanes and automobiles. We should be happy for the chance to say or do something that makes someone else happy. And we should do things that make us happy, intentionally and regularly.

One of the ways I make myself happy is to make someone else happy. It usually doesn't cost much or take a lot of energy. But when I've made someone else happy, it makes me happy. And when I'm happy, I'm energetic, creative, and productive. Deepak Chopra put it this way: "When we choose actions that bring happiness and success to others, the fruit of our karma is happiness and success."

Happiness is not a destination, it's a way to travel.

Do happy people have problems? Of course. But even as they are dealing with their problems, they appreciate the good things in the world around them and take the time to enjoy the little things that others often don't even notice.

My happiness is about keeping things simple and enjoying every moment to the max. Life is fleeting. If we don't stop and smell the proverbial roses along the way, what will we have to reflect back on when we're at the end of our lives?

Certainly not everything that makes me happy is simple. Sometimes it's a challenging project that took a lot of hard work, but when it was done, when it came off exactly as I'd planned and I heard the applause, I was happy.

You've heard about people who keep a gratitude diary. Every day they write down what they're thankful for. Why not keep a happiness diary?

What do you do well?

A classic piece of career advice is to find something that you enjoy doing and figure out how to get paid for doing it. There's nothing wrong with that, but it doesn't go far enough. Yes, you need to figure out what you enjoy, but it's also essential to identify what you're good at.

Just because you enjoy doing something doesn't mean you'll be good at it. If your stars are going to align, you need to spend most of your time doing things you enjoy *and* do well.

Figuring out what you like and do well can be a challenge because you may not have the opportunity to check out new things. How will you know if you like something and can do it if you don't try it? A good first step is to take a career aptitude and assessment test. You may be surprised at the results, and you may get some ideas you hadn't thought of.

It's okay to spend your spare time doing things you may not be especially good at but that you enjoy. You might enjoy playing a musical instrument, but you'll never do it well enough to make a living as a musician. You might enjoy playing a particular sport for recreation, but you'll never make it as a professional athlete—I know a lot of amateur golfers who fall into that category. That's okay. But for your career, whether you're an entrepreneur or you work for someone else, you need to find something that you're good at and that you *want* to do. The two things feed on each other.

In Chapter 2, we talked about drive. It's difficult if not impossible to maintain an inner drive to do something all day, every day if you don't do it well. You can try it, but it's like climbing an enormous mountain that somehow keeps growing higher and steeper. It's much easier to develop drive and ambition to pursue a goal when you enjoy what you're doing *and* you do it well.

What is your purpose?

If you've taken some basic business courses, you've probably studied how companies define their purpose and mission. It's a similar process when you do it for yourself. Your mission is *what* you do; your purpose is *why* you do it. You won't know what to do if you don't understand why you're doing it.

To figure out your purpose, ask yourself these questions:

What did I love doing as a child?
What do I love doing now?
What are my talents?
What comes easy to me?
What do other people thank me for?
What is my definition of success?
What issues do I care most about?
Who are my mentors and why?
When have I experienced the greatest joy?
What makes me forget to eat?

If I only had one year to live, what would I do?
How do I want to be remembered?

Use the answers to those questions to guide you as you define your purpose. After you've articulated your purpose—your why— in your mind, write it down. Study it. Be sure you real-

> *How much intensity are you willing to muster up to achieve your goal?*

ly mean it. Then use it to guide your planning for what you're going to do in life. Refer to it regularly so you stay on track and spend your time doing things that will help you live your purpose.

Go all in

Whatever you do, whatever motivates you, give it one hundred percent. Function with total intensity. Go all in. The only way to live without regrets is to give it your all, every time, win, lose, or draw.

You've heard the term "super laser-focused"—that's intensity. That's what it takes to achieve great things. When you see professional athletes winning games, breaking records, doing incredible things, it's all about intensity. The question you have to ask yourself is: How much intensity are you willing to muster up to achieve your goal? I believe you have the intensity you need inside of you right now—your job is to discover it and determine what to use it for.

Homework

List three people you admire (living or dead) who understood their purpose from a young age and lived it their entire lives. What can you learn from them?

_____

_____

_____

_____

_____

_____

_____

_____

_____

_____

_____

_____

_____

Figure out your purpose and write it down. Use the questions on page 36 to help you.

_____

_____

_____

_____

_____

_____

_____

List the things you enjoy doing and the things you do well. Identify where those things merge.

Identify at least one thing that is stopping you from going all in and figure out what you can do about it.

Do something today that will make someone else happy.

CHAPTER FOUR

CHAPTERS OF LIFE

We're not going to live forever. When we're young, we don't think about that much. As we get older, we become increasingly aware of the reality that more of our life is behind us than is ahead of us. Especially in our culture, there's something about turning 50 that makes us do some serious self-examination. I've found that I'm more philosophical now that I'm past 50.

Maturity brings with it an understanding of where you're supposed to be, what you're supposed to be doing, who you're supposed to be doing it with. The great teacher that is experience helps us learn from successes, failures, and even simple interactions—and not only learn, but become better for it.

Life is like a book that's divided into chapters. You might consider your first chapter from birth until you start school. Then chapter two would be elementary, middle, and high school. Chapter three might be college and graduate school. Chapter four could be when you get married and have kids. Chapter five is your career. And then there's the chapter of what's next. This is when you start trying to figure out how your story is going to end. Some people refer to this as the midlife crisis, but it doesn't have to be a crisis. For some people, of course, it is—they decide they're not happy and they do stupid things. Others realize they need to make changes while they still have time. Good for them. They've figured it out. And still others recognize that they're on the right track and just need to keep going.

What you need to do to live out your purpose will vary depending on where you are in life. Successful people know how to make their stars align at different stages of their lives. What they needed to do in their thirties was different than what they'll need to do in their sixties or older. Generally, you can take more risks when you're younger because you have time to recover if you make a mistake, particularly in the areas of finances and career choices. As you get older, you may become more cautious—or you may decide to throw caution to the wind and take chances while you still can. Ultimately everyone has the same fate: Death is the final chapter of our lives. But before we reach that last page, we have the opportunity at every step to evaluate what we're doing, to reflect on our successes and failures, to think about what has brought us great joy and what hasn't. If we're not satisfied, we can change the course of this journey of life.

Though you can make changes as you go, you can't skip any of the chapters of your life. You can't fast-forward to see how it ends. You have to live every day of every chapter. You won't enjoy all of it, but you have to do it. You have to keep going.

Counting the days

We've talked about life in terms of chapters. Now I'm going to put it in a different perspective. Let's look at life in terms of days.

The first 20 years of your life is 7,300 days. For most of us, those are days primarily consumed by learning. You're born, you learn to walk and talk, you go to school, you might learn to play a sport or a musical instrument, you start college. You might have a job while you're in school—another learning experience. So that's the first 7,300 days of your life.

Going from when you're 20 until you're 50 years old is 30 years. That's about 11,000 days. During those days, you might finish college, go to work, develop a career. You could get married, have kids, buy a house, start a business—those are all the kinds of things that typically happen to us during the 11,000 days between the time we're 20 and 50.

> *Use your time wisely. Don't waste it. You only have so many days, and you need to make sure each one counts.*

Then you hit 50. You've lived more than 18,000 days. At best, your life is half over (unless you are one of those rare people who live past 100). It's time to take stock of how you've used your days so far and how you'll use the ones you have left.

For most people, the decade between 50 and 60 is

their prime earning years. That's 3,600 days of economic prime time—what are you going to do with those days?

Suddenly you're 60. You've been on this planet almost 22,000 days. You're starting to think about how much longer you're going to work—maybe even how much longer you're going to live. You're thinking about your health, your lifestyle, your DNA, where you live, your financial situation. Do you want to stop working? If so, can you afford to? What will you do with the days you have left?

When you're young, the days pass slowly. You think you're going to live forever—if you even think about that at all. But when you hit your 40s and 50s, time begins to speed up. By the time you hit 60, everything is happening at warp speed.

As someone who is over 50, I've started thinking about how much time I have left. I've lived more than 17,000 days. Most of them have been good days, full of excitement and adventure and great experiences. But what's left? How many more days do I have to do the things I enjoy, to spend with the people I love? I don't know. None of us do.

It's an interesting perspective when you think about life in terms of days. The process puts a spotlight on the value of time. We're going to talk more about time in Chapter 6, but for now, know how important it is to use your time wisely. Don't waste it. You only have so many days, and you need to make sure each one counts.

Retire or not?

I'm not afraid of many things, but retirement is something

I fear. The day that I'm not running my company, what will I be doing? Right now, I don't know.

Some people work all their lives building up to the retirement crescendo. It's something they've looked forward to for years. Others think retirement sounds morbid, like it's the end of their lives. They hear "retirement" and think "tired"—and it's not something they want.

Retirement means something different to everyone. Is retirement a time in space? Is retirement a psychological place? Is retirement an economic reality? Is it a medical reality? What is retirement?

I challenge everyone to define retirement in their own way. What does retirement mean to you? Understanding that will help you on your life's journey. You'll be able to plan better, to make smarter decisions. But even though you should be thinking about retirement long before you're ready to do it, don't postpone living your life until you retire. Enjoy life while you're working. If your stars are aligned, that's easy to do.

If retirement is defined as the time in our lives when we are no longer required to work, I can say that I live like I'm retired right now. I'm doing what I choose to do. I don't do it because I *have* to; I do it because I *want* to. I am financially secure whether I'm working or not. But there may come a time when I don't want to run my company anymore. When that happens, I'm not sure how I'll spend my time. Knowing how you'll spend your time when you're not going to work every day is a key part of retirement planning.

Even as I tell you that you need to prepare yourself for retirement, I'm struggling to do the same. I know that

I don't want to own my business when I die, but right now I don't have a timeframe for how much longer I want to work. Something else I think about—and if you own a business, you should consider this, too—is that if you die when you're actively running a business, you may be creating a burden for your family. Especially if your family is not involved in your business, they may not know how to deal with it. And while they're trying to figure it out, the business will likely suffer. It's not easy to do when you're busy running the show, but you should have a succession plan in place so your business will survive when you're no longer running it.

Truly driven entrepreneurs don't understand retirement. Someone could pay them a large sum of money to buy their company, but they'd be bored without having to do the work of running their business. And many entrepreneurs won't even consider selling their businesses because that's what provides them with purpose. This attitude is also common with entrepreneurial employees—those leaders

Being independent means you are self-sufficient, you know how to make good decisions, and you are free to choose your relationships, associates, and lifestyle.

at all levels who may not own the company but who are as committed to it as if they do.

If you're going to sell your business (or cash out your savings and investments) and retire, consider spending some of your time working in a philanthropic effort so you can use your expertise and see results, but still be out of your business. Bill Gates is a great example of how to do that. He spends most of his time giving away his money—but he doesn't just write checks, he's involved in the things he cares about. Of course, very few of us will ever operate on that scale, but the principle still applies.

What makes people want to continue working when they have whatever resources they need to live the rest of their lives in a manner that they find comfortable? It's because work provides them with a way to live out their purpose. As we discussed in Chapter 3, people need purpose and direction. Without it, they're lost.

You can only go on so many vacations. You can only buy so many toys. You can only play so many rounds of golf. When it's all over, you want to know that your life meant something. That's why long before the time comes that you retire and sell your business or hand it down to your children or whatever, you need to think about how that's going to change your life and what you're going to do to continue living out your purpose.

A friend of mine who is very wealthy tells me he doesn't need any more money, but he continues to work because he loves creating opportunities for his employees. He could piddle along and do nothing for the rest of his life and never run out of money, but he's still growing his business because he enjoys seeing the people who work with him be successful. I admire that.

At this stage of my life, I recognize that I want to run my company as long as it's fun. When it's not fun, I won't do it anymore. I'll find something else to do.

The importance of independence

I was independent from a young age. I always wanted to do my own thing and take responsibility for myself. Being independent helps you grow and evolve; it helps you get the most out of every day of your life. The younger you are when you develop independence, the more time you have to appreciate its benefits.

Let's define independence. Independence means you can survive on your own. You can develop and sustain a lifestyle of your choosing. You have freedom, and you can make your own choices. Of course, independence comes with a cost. You may have to make some sacrifices, but when you're independent, it's your choice. The more independent you are, the more choices you have.

Being independent does *not* mean being alone. It does *not* mean you exist without relationships that are important to you. It does *not* mean you are never part of a team. It means you are self-sufficient, you know how to make good decisions, and you are free to choose your relationships, associates, and lifestyle.

One of the most important things you do as an independent person is learn to swim—and I say this both literally and metaphorically. One of the first things parents do—or should do—is teach their babies to swim. The first few times in the water, the baby will scream and cry, and the parents will feel horrible. But what have they done? The baby has learned how to survive if he falls into the water. The baby has learned a degree of independence.

We are not born independent. Babies are totally dependent on their parents and other caregivers. Similarly, we are often not independent toward the end of our lives. As we age, we may find ourselves needing help with things we used to be able to do on our own. This is part of the natural cycle of life—that when we're very young and very old, we have to depend on others. But for all those years in between, be independent.

Habits

A habit is something we do regularly without giving it much thought—but our habits define us in ways we probably don't realize. We begin developing habits from infancy and continue acquiring and modifying habits throughout the chapters of our lives.

We all have habits that we consider bad—or at least, not good. A bad habit is a repetitive negative behavior that could range from annoying (such as nail biting, chewing on a pen, fidgeting, interrupting) to harmful (such as overspending, procrastinating, smoking). We also all have good habits—positive things we do routinely, such as getting a good night's rest, taking vitamins, flossing our teeth, exercising, eating right.

Habits affect our happiness and the outcomes of our lives. They can both help and hinder our efforts to get our stars aligned. They can also mean the difference between achieving our goals or failing. Unfortunately, most people don't recognize their good and bad habits and the impact of their habits on their lives.

Does that mean if you have a bunch of bad habits you should just give up? No. We have the ability to change our habits, to either simply stop a bad habit (very difficult to do) or replace it with a good one (a better approach).

The challenge is that there is no one-size-fits-all solution for ending bad habits and creating good ones. In fact, there are thousands of ways to change habits for the better. For example, if you're trying to break a smoking habit, do breathing exercises when the urge to light up hits. Or if you're trying to spend less time on social media, force yourself to do something productive first, and be specific about what that must be. Maybe you have a habit of interrupting people. Ask a trusted friend or colleague to monitor you and give you a signal when you've interrupted; or, when you feel yourself getting ready to speak over someone else, take a drink of water.

It's important to figure out what triggers your bad habits and elimiate those triggers. For example, if you overeat when you're bored or stressed, learn to recognize those feelings and come up with an alternative behavior. If a certain location or environment triggers a bad habit, figure out how to either avoid that place or change the environment.

Do what works for you so you can create a foundation of positive, heathy habits that will allow you to get and keep your stars aligned.

Homework

How many days have you lived? Analyze how you've used your days so far and how you'll use the ones you have ahead of you.

_____

_____

_____

_____

_____

_____

_____

_____

_____

_____

_____

_____

_____

Think about what retirement might look like for you.

_____

_____

_____

_____

_____

_____

_____

_____

Make a list of three bad habits you have and a plan to change them.

_____
_____
_____
_____
_____
_____
_____
_____
_____
_____

Make a list of three good habits you'd like to have and a plan to develop them.

_____
_____
_____
_____
_____
_____
_____
_____
_____
_____
_____

CHAPTER FIVE

CHARACTERISTICS SUCCESSFUL PEOPLE SHARE

When you look at people you consider successful, you'll see that they share a lot of the same characteristics. While some of these traits are innate in their personalities, successful people work to develop most of them.

The characteristics we're going to discuss in this chapter are by no means all the ones successful people have in common, but they are the most important. If you work on cultivating these traits in yourself, achieving success will come much easier for you.

Successful people are confident

We're not born with confidence. We develop it with

experience. Confidence comes with honing our skills, increasing our knowledge, and achieving small successes that lead to larger ones. Did you have any confidence in your ability to ride the first time you got on a bike? Of course not. But once you learned how and practiced, you were able to hop on a bike and pedal away without even thinking about what you were doing. You were confident.

When I talk about confidence, I'm talking about genuine confidence, not fake-it-'til-you-make-it bravado. I think most of us can tell when someone is genuinely confident, when they truly know what they're talking about, or if they're just a BS artist. Confidence is an inalienable thing no one can take away from you. You either have it or you don't. And if you don't, you need to develop it.

Confidence was one of the most important things I had going for me in my early days in the entertainment technology business.

Closed-circuit satellite events were popular then—it was long before cable, pay-per-view, and live-streaming services. Promoters would make their events available on a satellite feed, and venues (typically convention centers, arenas, and large hotels) would pay a fee to access the feed. Then they would use a rented projector and freelance operator to show the event on a big screen in their facility and charge admission. The promoters made money on selling tickets, the venues made money on renting space as well as food and beverage sales, and companies like mine made money renting the equipment—and customers got to see live events.

One of the most popular closed-circuit satellite events was boxing. When I was 18, I went to see Phil Alessi, who was a boxing promoter in Tampa. He also owned Alessi Bakeries, but his first love was boxing. He wanted to promote a number of closed-circuit boxing events, and I wanted the contract to provide the equipment and operators. Of course, he wasn't going to just hand over a $50,000 deposit check to a kid who claimed to know the business. I had to convince him that I could do the work— even though I hadn't yet done a job of that size. I had to make him trust and believe in me. I was able to do that because I was confident in my abilities and it showed. He signed the contract and gave me a check.

At the time, my company was new and this was the biggest check I'd received—a $50,000 deposit on a $100,000 contract. When I took it to the bank, I was the happiest kid you ever met. I still had to perform, and I did. And Phil Alessi was a customer for a long time.

Confidence is more than just a good thing to have— in business, it's essential. Think about it: Why would you buy from anyone who isn't confident in their product and

The perils of overconfidence

There's confidence—and then there's over-confidence. And being over-confident can be just as damaging as being under-confident.

People want to work with people who are confident but not cocky. Over-confidence is likely to come across as cocky, and that can send the wrong message. It can be a turnoff. It can make people think that you're so impressed with yourself that you don't have time for them and their project. You need to find that line between attractive confidence and offensive cockiness.

service? And if you wouldn't buy from someone who lacks confidence, why would anyone buy from you if you lack confidence, if you can't convince them that you're the solution to their problem? Genuinely confident people are secure in who they are and what they can do. They're not easily intimidated.

Let's clarify the difference between fake-it-'til-you-make-it and being confident you can do something you haven't done before. My policy is: Don't fake it. Be honest. There are people who will say they can do anything and try to figure it out later. Sometimes that works, but it doesn't always. It's risky, and the damage it can do to your reputation isn't worth it.

Instead of saying or implying that you've done something you haven't, tell the truth: "We haven't done that before, but I believe we can and here's why" then tell them why. That's something you would want to know as an educated buyer, right? If you wouldn't want someone to lie to you, why would you do it to your customers? Whatever we do, whether as an individual or a company, there's a first time for doing it. People will understand if you've never done anything exactly like what you're pitching if you're

Confidence can change performance

Not only will confidence help you in your relationships, but it can also improve your performance. It lets you walk into situations without doubts or trepidations—it gives you more pep in your step.

When people challenge me, my confidence is what drives me to know that I can perform at the highest level. It's something inside me that no one can take away.

prepared to answer all their questions about why and how you can do it.

The other side of this is learning to see people for who they really are and not for whatever persona they're trying to assume. How can you tell if someone is the real thing? It takes a little investment. Depending on the situation, you may ask for examples of when they have done what you're discussing. Or you may want to verify what they said with another expert. Sometimes you'll just depend on your intuition.

There will be times when someone will ask a question you can't answer, even about something you have a great deal of experience with. Don't try to bluff your way through it. The really smart, confident people are comfortable admitting that they don't know and promising to find out. And you'll earn greater respect for your honesty. Just be sure you follow through.

Take pride in yourself

Pride is a subset of confidence. Pride is defined as "a feeling or deep pleasure or satisfaction derived from one's own achievements, the achievements of those with whom one is closely associated, or from qualities or possessions that are widely admired." (It's also the term used for a group of lions forming a social unit, but that's not the kind of pride we're talking about here.)

We all have some degree of pride. We develop pride from experience, from the times when we've performed well, from when we've received applause and compliments. We all want to be proud of what we do and who we do it with. As a leader, you have a responsibility to create an organization that will allow your people to feel a sense of pride in the company and their coworkers. And to do that, you need to take pride in the organization yourself. You can't cut corners or rip people off. You need to deliver quality products and services. You need to do the right thing by your employees. When you build pride among your people, in addition to creating a team of high-performers, you also build loyalty.

Pride is also related to ego, which we'll discuss more in Chapter 8.

Balance pride with humility

A companion quality to pride is humility, which is the quality of being humble. It means to be modest, to think of others before yourself, not to have an over-inflated idea of your own importance. Successful people know how to balance pride and humility. For example, suppose a customer compliments you on the job your company did. A normal reaction would be to accept it by saying "Thank you" and moving on with the conversation. A more thoughtful response would be to express your thanks and give credit to everyone who did the work. Say something like, "I'm fortunate to work with some of the most talented people in the business and they're the ones who make our service possible." That's a demonstration of humility.

One of the best examples of humility in the non-profit world is the anonymous donor. There's nothing wrong with taking public credit for donations, but the person who gives in secret is truly humble.

There are times when I exercise a lot of humility and other times—being completely honest—not so much.

When I'm in a competitive situation and talking about
my company and what we can do, I'm not humble. I'm
confident and proud. I know we're the best and I say so.
That's being strategic because I want my competitors to
be intimidated and my customers to be impressed. But I
know I'm not a one-man show. We have a team of hundreds
of people, and LMG and the ETP companies couldn't do
what they do without those dedicated folks.

Stay focused

Success requires focus and focus leads to great things.
Focus is essential from two perspectives.

The first is your overall life focus—what you are going to concentrate on in your life. For example, there are
a lot of talented athletes who are good at multiple sports,
but most of the ones who achieve professional success
pick one sport and focus on it. A lot of entrepreneurs have
ideas for multiple businesses, but most successful business
owners only have one business at a time. While there are
exceptions, most of us find it difficult to excel at a bunch
of different things at once.

The second perspective is focusing on the task at
hand. This is what you do with your time. Our lives are
a collection of distractions and confusion—emails, phone
calls, texts, social media, interruptions, employee issues,
family issues, and so on. I often joke that my life is just
a bunch of meetings in between distractions. But when
something is important, you have to focus on it and ignore
the distractions. You have to give it your full attention
and energy. This is one of my biggest challenges because
my business has a million moving parts and even when

I know I need to focus on one thing, there are dozens of others that need my attention.

Some people are linear and others are great multi-taskers. By linear, I mean that they need to start something and stick with it until it's complete. Multitaskers, on the other hand, can easily move between projects. They can start working on something, handle an interruption, then get back to the first project and continue forging ahead. There's nothing inherently wrong with being linear, but entrepreneurs have to be both linear and strong multitaskers. We have to be able to quickly shift our focus when circumstances require our immediate attention and then pick up where we left off. We have to be able to give people the direction they need without making them wait so they can get the job done. Think about what it would be like to a be a newspaper editor with dozens of story ideas coming at you and you've got to decide which ones you should run and which ones you shouldn't. Then you've got to make sure all the articles are edited, checked, typeset, and placed on the appropriate pages. And it all has to get done on schedule so the newspaper can to get on the press in time to be printed and put on the delivery trucks so the papers are in the hands of readers on schedule. That's the ultimate multitasking. And then you do it all over again the next day. Newspaper editors have to be able to jump from one task to another to another and back again—and know where they are at all times. So do entrepreneurs.

Of course, when something is a top priority, you need to have the focus and discipline to stick to it until it's done. That's when you need to be linear.

When you have focus, you have the ability to keep

your eye on the prize, you know how to manage distractions, you do what you say and deliver on time.

Energy = Action

I have a nickname at work—they call me plutonium. I'm definitely a high-energy person, and all of the successful people I know are also high-energy. Energy is the strength and vitality you need to accomplish whatever physical or mental activity you want to do.

Success is about getting things done—not talking but doing. It's planning and execution. You can't be successful without energy because you need energy for action. Simply put, high-energy people accomplish more.

High energy is positive. It helps when you're trying to persuade people, whether you're selling or managing a team. Like a positive attitude, positive energy can be contagious. I prefer working *People who have high energy are the ones that rule the world.* with high-energy people and I think most people do, as well. People who have high energy are the ones that rule the world.

Of course, people are different. Not everyone is high-energy. And even high-energy people sometimes get depleted. On an energy scale of 1 to 10, if you're not at least a consistent 5 and preferably higher, you need to figure out why not and fix it. I understand that for many people, that's much easier to say than do, but it's not healthy to be low-energy. Low-energy people miss out on so much in life. It's hard for them to do what it takes to get their stars aligned.

If you're low-energy, could it be from something as simple as boredom? For example, if you're doing a job you hate or that doesn't challenge you, it will affect your energy and your attitude. People in that situation often go from low-energy to high-energy quickly when they can spend their time doing something they care about that excites them. For many people, the cause of low energy is more complex. It could be a health issue; see a doctor and get checked out. If you're suffering from depression, get help through medication and counseling. If your diet and exercise regimen is poor, put together a plan to improve so you can get in shape. If your energy level fluctuates, figure out what you need to do to maintain it more consistently.

My point is not to offer overly-simplistic solutions to a complicated problem—it's to stress that a trait successful people share is being high-energy. Do whatever it takes to boost your energy and watch your life change for the better.

Make the commitment

In Chapter 3, we talked about going all in. That's what commitment means. If we're going to work on something together, I want to know if you're all in. And if you're only sort of in, or maybe in, I'm going to look for someone else. When it comes to my business, I have total commitment. I'm also totally committed to certain things outside my business—I'm

> *I've always been totally all in when it comes to my company but I've never lost sight of the importance of my family and balancing my work and home life.*

committed to my family, to my health, to my friends. And you can see that commitment in what I say and, more importantly, what I do.

Here's an example of how commitment manifests in my life: I had a personal trainer for ten years. His name was Frank Chandler—he not only was a great trainer, but he also introduced me to my wife. When you pay a personal trainer to work out with you, you've made a commitment. I paid him in advance, and I knew I had to show up or else I was throwing my money away.

But what if you don't have a personal trainer and you still go to the gym regularly? I think that shows an even greater commitment to why you work out, which is to stay strong and healthy, to look good, to keep your energy level high. When you make a promise to do something and the only person who loses if you don't follow through is you, you've demonstrated commitment.

Beyond the characteristic of commitment, you need to decide what you're going to commit to because that connects to your values and how you spend your time. Commitment is about making choices. Sometimes they're easy; sometimes they're hard. You have the choice of sleeping in or going to the gym. You have the choice of doing volunteer work or blowing it off. You have the choice of taking classes to earn a degree and improve your leadership skills, or you can spend your evenings watching television. You have the choice of doing the right thing by your employees by spending the extra money or making the effort to create a work environment that will allow them to be their best, or you can cut corners and just hire new people when your employees leave because they don't feel valued.

It's important to recognize that we can be committed at different levels to different things throughout our lives, depending on where we are. For example, you may have been totally committed to earning an advanced degree; once you've got it, you'll find something else to commit to, such as getting a job commensurate with your new credentials. You may have been committed to getting a promotion; again, once you've got it, you'll find new goals to work on. Or you may have made a commitment to a company or a cause and the leadership makes some changes you don't agree with—that can change your commitment level. Certainly, my personal and social commitments changed after I got married and again after we had kids.

There are three places where my commitment has always been total and never changed: My commitment to always do the right thing, my commitment to my business, and my commitment to my family. While my goals have evolved, I've always been totally all in when it comes to my company, but I've never lost sight of the importance of my family and balancing my work and home life. This balance is what keeps my energy high and allows me to consistently function at my best. And most of the successful people I know who are well-rounded and happy are the same way.

When demonstrating commitment, you connect in a special way to the person or cause you're committed to—and then great things can happen. If you can't be totally committed to something, let it go. Don't be gray—be black and white. Be either in or out. Having the characteristic of commitment and demonstrating it in all aspects of your life will enrich you in ways you never dreamed possible.

Rise to the moment

When you have the chance to do something, especially something you've never done before, you need to rise to the moment. If you don't, the opportunity will probably be lost.

The ability to rise to the moment requires confidence, focus, energy, and commitment. This is most visible in sports, especially during playoffs and championship games. The superstar athletes ignore the crowd and focus on what they have to do to be their best and make that game-winning shot. Even though it may not be in the spotlight, the need to rise to the moment happens to entrepreneurs regularly. Something unexpected presents itself and you either rise to the occasion and seize the opportunity, or you let it pass you by.

When we were asked to provide the visual elements— the LED floor for the stage and projection mapping the stadium floor—for the 2012 Super Bowl halftime show with Madonna, it meant doing something that hadn't been done before. We had to figure out how to align multiple video projectors at 150 feet in the air above the field. Even more challenging was that it had to be done under strict time constraints—seven minutes to set it up, a twelve-minute show, then five minutes to strike the equipment so the game could resume. We had to perform at our highest level in a limited amount of time in front of an audience of more than 100 million viewers. To figure it out, we brought in resources and expertise. We ran tests on the grounds outside of our office. We did what we had to do to make sure we could deliver, and we were successful. We rose to the occasion. And it helped us capture new clients.

It's easy to get into a routine, to do what's safe and predictable. That can bring you a measure of security and even some success. But if you're going to win the proverbial championship, you need to react quickly when those once-in-a-lifetime opportunities present themselves. Always be ready to rise to the moment.

If you're going to win the proverbial championship, you need to react quickly when those once-in-a-lifetime opportunities present themselves.

Be comfortable with being uncomfortable

You've probably heard the term *comfort zone*. It's a place or situation where we feel at ease and safe, with no stress or anxiety. While it's certainly a place that feels good, successful people don't spend a lot of time there. Successful people are comfortable being uncomfortable. They're comfortable with the unfamiliar, with trying new things that will allow them to grow.

When I'm in the uncomfortable zone, I stretch it to make it comfortable. By that, I mean I figure out what's going on and what I need to learn and do to achieve the goals of the situation.

Years ago, when LMG was much smaller, we made our first large purchase of LED screens from a company in Korea. We were dealing with a middleman, a U.S. vendor that we thought had an exclusive contract with the manufacturer, but it turned out that they didn't. We realized that we not only could but should be buying directly from the manufacturer in Korea. Back then, we were spending hundreds of thousands of dollars (today it's millions) annually with companies in China, but we didn't know how to do business with them because we weren't familiar with their customs and how they operated. We were outside of our comfort zone.

At the time, we weren't comfortable flying across the world to countries where we didn't know people and didn't speak the language to build relationships we needed to be really successful. We made some initial mistakes in the process but we eventually learned, and today we have many successful relationships with Asian-based companies. Negotiating directly with them has ultimately saved us millions of dollars. This knowledge is one of the things that has allowed us to grow and develop relationships with many other suppliers which has contributed to our success.

If we had stayed in our comfort zone and continued purchasing from brokers, we would have been overpaying for our products, and that would have put us at a competitive disadvantage. Getting out of our comfort zone paid off in a big way. I've found it usually does.

Think about the first time you did something like diving into a pool, riding a bicycle, or even making a presentation at work. Even though you may have prepared and been coached on how to do it, you were probably very uncomfortable. Then you did it. Maybe it went perfectly, maybe it didn't, but either way, you expanded your comfort zone.

Les M. Goldberg

Being uncomfortable can mean the opportunity to achieve something great. Try new things, gain new experiences, deal with people you may not have dealt with before—that's when you grow.

Homework

Have you ever had the experience of confidence improving your performance? If so, how can you duplicate that experience?

_____

_____

_____

_____

_____

_____

_____

_____

_____

List everything that makes you proud of your company (either the one you own or the one you work for).

_____

_____

_____

_____

_____

_____

_____

_____

_____

_____

_____

List three things you can do in the next two weeks to boost your energy.

_____
_____
_____
_____
_____
_____
_____

What are you committed to? Make a list of the things in your personal and professional life that you are totally committed to.

_____
_____
_____
_____
_____
_____
_____
_____
_____
_____
_____
_____
_____

When was the last time you got out of your comfort zone? What did you learn?

_____

_____

_____

_____

_____

_____

_____

_____

_____

_____

_____

_____

CHAPTER SIX

REALITY OF SUCCESS

Success doesn't happen by accident. You have to prepare for it. You have to be watching for opportunities. And when those opportunities come your way, you have to be ready to take advantage of them. How many times have you heard about a successful business that grew too fast and then crashed and burned because it couldn't produce enough product or meet customer demands? The problem wasn't that the business grew too fast; it was that the owner and managers weren't prepared for success. Do you see the difference?

Dealing with success is not always easy—in fact, it's almost always challenging. There is an infinite number of moving parts to a successful business, whether it's a small mom-and-pop operation or a large corporation or something in between. For your stars to align so that you can achieve and enjoy success, you must understand the reality of it and be ready to manage it.

The first thing you have to do to prepare for success is to know what it is. How do you define success? In my mind, success is doing what you want to do, when you want to do it, how you want to do it and, in the process, achieve a level of pride and sense of accomplishment which results in happiness. Success might be something else for you.

Some people use money or other material ways to measure success—how much they earn, how much their net worth is, how big their company is, what kind of house they live in or car they drive. That's fine, but it's not all there is. I've discovered that the true rewards and the real satisfaction of success come when you take money out of the equation. Your definition of success might include public accolades, such as receiving awards in your industry or being recognized as a thought leader. It

Success is doing what you want to do, when you want to do it, how you want to do it and, in the process, achieve a level of pride and sense of accomplishment which results in happiness.

might be building a company that creates jobs and contributes to the economy. Whatever it is, you need to know it so you can be ready for it.

As you consider what success means to you, keep this in mind: Every successful person has had their share of failure. Often that failure has helped them clarify their definition of success. In his book *The Heart of Leader*, Ken Blanchard wrote, "Success is not forever and failure isn't fatal."

Think of all the stories about people who have

gained and lost fortunes, then gained them again. After he became famous as the author of *The Adventures of Tom Sawyer*, Mark Twain made some bad investments. Destitute and bankrupt, he moved his family to Europe, went on a speaking tour and wrote prolifically, and eventually made enough money to restore his fortune and repay his debts.

Country music artist Willie Nelson's tax problems were widely publicized. When he couldn't pay, the feds took everything he owned, including real estate in several states, most of his instruments, recordings, and memorabilia. He went back to work and is as successful as ever today. Nelson once said, "There are more serious problems in life than financial ones, and I've had a lot of those. I've been broke before, and will be again."

Even Walt Disney had his troubles. His first company, an animation and film studio in Kansas City, failed in 1922. You know that his next venture, Disney Bros. Studio in California, did better.

Two of the most important lessons you can take from these stories and others like them are:

One, sometimes what looks like a setback is really a good setup for your next chapter of growth. Vince Lombardi put it well when he said, "The greatest accomplishment is not in never falling, but in rising again after you fall."

Two, even though you may know what success is for you, you can't just sit back and wait for it to happen and then coast through it. I'll repeat: You have to prepare for it. And when your preparations begin to show results and good things start happening, you need to be prepared to take advantage of them. If you don't know how to respond to the opportunity that is all around us, you'll never achieve success; you'll just plod along for the rest of your life.

Let's talk about what you can do to prepare for and deal with the reality of success.

Surround yourself with successful people

A quote usually attributed to the late Jim Rohn that we've all heard is: "You're the average of the five people you spend the most time with." I think it goes further than that. You are a reflection of *all* the people you surround yourself with.

My closest friends are mostly successful business or professional people. Some are more successful and wealthier than I am, some are not. All are people I have a lot in common with, that I enjoy spending time with. The friendships are genuine. I don't use people and I'm not suggesting that you should. But it's human nature that we tend to become like those with whom we associate. How many times have you heard people talk about someone who "fell into the wrong crowd" and got into trouble? Interesting how people blame associates for bad behavior but don't credit them for good. Try "falling in with the right crowd" and see what happens.

I'm going to talk more about relationships in Chapter 7, but when it comes to success, your relationships are critical.

The truth about luck

You've heard the old saying that luck is when preparation

meets opportunity. It's absolutely true. But—as with so many other things—there's more to it than that. There's luck and there's dumb luck. Dumb luck is an accident. It doesn't require any skill or strategy. It's winning the lottery. It's being in the right place at the right time when you didn't plan it or work for it.

What many people think of as luck (not dumb luck) is really preparation and hard work. I know people look at me and say that I'm lucky because I have a successful company, I travel in my private plane, I go on great vacations, and I enjoy the other material trappings of success. People who think that way don't have a genuine understanding of what I did to get where I am. They don't understand luck.

If you apply for a job at Zappos, one of the interview

Getting there is most of the fun

For successful people, life in general and business in particular is about what I call the thrill of the kill. Of course, I'm not talking about actually killing anything, I'm talking about having the desire and the energy to achieve your goals while you love every minute of the process. Some people call it the thrill of the hunt. It's what provides people with adrenaline, it's what fuels their purpose with the energy to accomplish things, it's what keeps them going every day. I appreciate everything that goes into figuring out how to give our customers what they want every bit as much as I enjoy watching the results of all that hard work.

Success is not a specific point in time, it's a journey. Enjoy every step of it.

questions you'll be asked is: "On a scale of one to ten, how lucky are you?" People who don't consider themselves lucky aren't a fit with the company's culture. Though the company's CEO Tony Hsieh says they want to hire lucky people who will bring more good luck to Zappos, the question was inspired by a study showing that people who perceived themselves to be lucky outperformed people who didn't. We all have the ability to make ourselves lucky with the right attitude, positive thinking, and proper preparation for whatever we're doing or whatever we want.

Is there such a thing as true luck, where something good happened and it was just a fluke? Or you avoided something bad by pure chance? Sure. Think about the casino game of roulette. Whether you win or lose at roulette is just a fluke. There's no science, no skill involved—it's just luck. And though it might be fun to play the game for a few minutes or even hours, you can't base your probability of life and business success on true luck. If you happen to get lucky, great. But you're going to achieve more and do it faster by working both smart and hard so that you are ready for whatever circumstances you happen to encounter.

Risks and rewards

Success involves risks, and often the potential reward is in direct proportion to the risk you take.

If you want the rewards, you have to take risks. In Chapter 2, I shared the story of when the Cleveland Cavaliers took the risk of contracting with us for the equipment and technical team for their victory parade, knowing there was a chance the parade wouldn't happen. But they were willing to take the risk of paying to have us in place for the parade because they were confident in their team's ability and they wanted that world-class celebration ready in Cleveland.

Before you take a risk, know what the reward will be. Know what you can achieve. And know what the consequences will be if you fail. To use a baseball analogy, you won't hit a home run every time you're at bat—in fact, you won't even hit the ball every time you swing. But if you never step into the batter's box, it's a guarantee that you won't score.

Nothing great is ever achieved without a certain amount of risk. We could never have put a man on the moon without taking a risk. Life-changing medical discoveries such as vaccines, antibiotics, and surgical procedures required risk. Risk is a component of putting yourself in a position of success.

But I'm not talking about foolish risks. I'm talking smart risks, calculated risks. Risks that have been well thought-out and mitigated as much as possible.

We all have a degree of risk-tolerance, a level of risk we're willing to accept. For example, you might go into a casino and say you're only going to gamble $100 and then you'll quit. Someone else might be willing to gamble $10,000. Of course, your economic circumstances play a large part in your risk tolerance—how much can you afford to lose? But there are other factors related to risk tolerance that vary by individual.

Though great risks can generate great rewards, they can also generate great losses. Risk-taking is not for everyone. In particular, it's hard to be an entrepreneur if you're not a risk-taker. And that's okay because entrepreneurs need employees. They need good people to help them build their companies. If everyone were an entrepreneur, we'd have no workers. So before you start a business, decide if you have what it takes to be the business owner or if you're better suited to work as a leader on someone else's team.

There are plenty of talented people out there who have entrepreneurial spirits but prefer to work for existing companies rather than start their own. I know because those are the kind of people who are on my leadership team. I have tremendous respect for their knowledge and abilities, and I depend on them to be entrepreneurial every day. You don't need to start the company to be a leader in it. Randall L. Stephenson, the chairman, CEO, and president of AT&T, started his career working for Southwestern Bell Telephone. He's never owned a business. Neither has Sheryl Sandberg, COO of Facebook, who happens to have a net worth of $1.6 billion. But they both have entrepreneurial spirits.

Words are powerful. The words you say, hear, and read have an impact on others and yourself.

If you want to be in business, whether you're starting your own or serving as an executive in a company, you need to know your risk tolerance and don't take risks when you are not willing and able to deal with the worst-case outcome. Let's say someone asks you to invest in a business deal. You need to study the proposal, review the business plan, consider who is involved, and evaluate a myriad of other issues before you can decide if you're willing to take the risk of investing.

If you own your company, every time you open a new location, try a new line of business, or invest in some new technology, you're engaging in risk. You're taking an action for which you have the chance to be either right or wrong. The degree to which you are right or wrong is the degree to which you succeed or fail. You might be extremely successful or only moderately so. Your failure might be a minimal loss or a major disaster. The key to dealing with risk is to mitigate as much as possible up front to reduce your ultimate exposure and be sure that exposure is manageable.

Speaking of failure, if you never fail, you haven't taken enough risk. Consider a bank that never makes bad loans. You could say they are the smartest bankers in the world, but more than likely they are so conservative with their lending practices that they're missing out on an abundance of profitable loans. Business involves good deals and bad deals. If you only go for the sure things, you won't have much to do. Be willing to take some risks; just do what you can to mitigate them.

Some of the biggest regrets people have come from not taking risks. Success requires risk. Be sure the rewards are greater than the risk and that you can manage the consequences if you fail.

Words matter

There's an adage you may have learned as a child that goes, "Sticks and stones may break my bones but words will never hurt me." Though the saying might help teach youngsters to ignore verbal bullying and insults, the reality is that it's not true. Words are powerful. Whether you're six or sixty, the words you say, hear, and read have an impact on others and yourself.

Think about it: We're still reading and being influenced by works that were authored thousands of years ago. Written words—books, articles, and so on—have an infinite lifespan. But the spoken word is not necessarily short-lived. Even when it's not recorded, it's remembered—often for generations.

I didn't always realize the power of words. When I was younger, I didn't realize how important it is to validate someone's hard work and effort. I didn't understand how easy it is to build someone up or tear them down with words. I learned from making mistakes, from saying the wrong thing at the wrong time, and from not understanding that once the words are said, you can't unsay them. I was fortunate to have a leadership team that taught me the importance of public praise and compliments. They wrangled me in to make sure I understood this—I didn't learn it on my own. But I know now that you can create enemies or allies very quickly, just by what you say. I've had people tell me that something I said made a huge difference in their lives—and often I don't remember saying it. Sometimes it was something I said intentionally; other times, it was something spontaneous.

Effective leaders understand the power of words. We all want the people on our team to have super strength, like when there's an accident and the person who normally couldn't pick up thirty pounds is lifting a car off someone. I'm talking figuratively here—we want people to be extraordinary in the ways that are necessary for their job.

The right words can make someone Herculean. The wrong words can be devastating because they can make people feel inadequate and incompetent—and if they *feel* that way, they will *be* that way. It's not what you want.

As a leader, three of the most important phrases you can say are "please," "thank you," and "I'm sorry." Those little words can be powerful because they let people know you respect and appreciate them. Some people never admit they're wrong because they think it's a sign of weakness. In reality, being able to take responsibility when you're wrong and apologize for your mistakes shows strength and will earn you far more respect than denial and excuses will.

As important as words are, there must be truth and sincerity behind them. And if you make a promise, you need to keep it. When you don't honor your commitments, at the very least, you lose credibility. At worst, you hurt people.

> *Three of the most important phrases you can say are "please," "thank you," and "I'm sorry."*

Your actions will validate what you say.

In our technology-driven world, so much of what we say these days is recorded—especially if you're a public figure, but often even if you're not. When your words are documented, it's easy to go back and see when your words didn't match your actions, when what you promised didn't line up with what you actually did. Your stars can only align if your words and deeds are also in alignment.

How do you spend your time?

In Chapter 3, we talked about what makes you happy.

Knowing what makes you happy is super important because that knowledge will drive how you spend your time. It's human nature that we will make time for the things that make us happy.

When people say, "I don't have time for that," what they're saying is, "That's not important to me." We make time for important things, essential things, things that matter to us.

In Chapter 4, we talked about the chapters of life from the perspective of an average lifespan. The reality is that we don't know how much time we have in this world. You could live to be 110, or you could get hit by a truck and die tomorrow. So use your time wisely.

You've heard the phrases "wasting time" and "killing time" as in, "I've got some time to kill." No, you don't! No one has time to kill. Think back to the concept of measuring your life in days—why would you want to waste even one of those days? Time is a non-renewable resource. Once it's gone, it's gone. Bruce Lee said, "If you love life, don't waste time, for time is what life is made up of." I couldn't agree more.

While time, in general, might be infinite, our own time is finite. Use it wisely, no matter what you're doing. Remember, time is non-refundable. Be present in the moments of your life, whether you're working, relaxing, spending time with your family, or whatever.

As important as it is to make your own time count, it's equally important to respect the time of others. Be punctual. You probably don't like to be kept waiting, so don't keep others waiting. If you're a manager, don't do things that cause your subordinates to spin their wheels.

When you have the opportunity, whether it's at work, home or elsewhere, teach people about the value of time.

From idea to reality

How to take a business idea and turn it into reality is a broad topic that's beyond the scope of this book, but it's an element of success that needs to be addressed.

Ideas are plentiful and cheap. It's the implementation that matters. I can't count the number of people I've met over the years who tell me they have a great idea, it's amazing, it's going to be a huge success—and it never comes to fruition. That's *When you have the opportunity, whether it's at work, home or elsewhere, teach people about the value of time.* because turning even the greatest idea into reality is like climbing Mount Everest. It's hard. It's risky. And not all of us have the resources to do it.

If you want to climb Mount Everest, there's a process you need to go through. You don't get to the top of the mountain in one leap. You need to get yourself physically ready for the climb. You need to have the money to pay for it (a guided trip up Everest can cost upwards of $70,000 plus airfare to Nepal, gear, and other expenses). You need to find and hire a guide service. The climb itself is done in stages. You have to get to the Everest Base Camp, then to Camp 1, Camp 2, Camp 3 and Camp 4 before you eventually reach the final summit. And then you have to get down.

Successful people who have an idea usually take the time to let it percolate through a process to come up with a plan for implementation. Sometimes that process reveals that what seemed like a great idea wasn't—it might need refining in some way or it might not work at all. For the ones that can work, the process identifies things like the degree of risk—some ideas are riskier than others. Some require more than others in terms of money, commitment, time, and effort. And the outcome is never guaranteed.

Creative people—as most entrepreneurs are—are going to have more ideas than they can ever possibly implement in a lifetime. That's fine because not every idea even the most successful people have is going to be a winner.

So what should you do when you have an idea for a product or a business? First, write it down. The exercise of writing your ideas down will help you determine their viability. If you can't get it in writing, you don't have a clear idea.

Next, create a plan for implementation. Sometimes you'll have what seemed like a fantastic idea but when you start working on it, you realize it isn't great as you thought, it won't work, it's not worth your time. As soon as you realize that, let it go. Move on to your next idea.

You should have at least a first draft of a plan in writing before you start talking to people or pitching your idea to investors. Do some market research. Is there a demand for what you want to do? Is your idea unique? Is anyone else already doing it and, if so, what will make your idea different enough to attract customers? Come up with some production estimates. What's it going to cost you to get up and running, to get your product to market? Figure out what resources you already have and what resources you're going to need. Is your idea still feasible?

If not, don't spend any more time on it. Go to work on something else. If it is, keep going. Refine your plan. Take it to your trusted advisors and get their opinion—do they think it's a great opportunity or a terrible idea? Get some real-world experience in the area of what you want to do. And when you feel like your plan is about ninety percent finished, begin the implementation process.

Finally, throughout this process, believe you can make it happen. If you don't believe in what you're doing, you've got a much harder hill to climb. It's not impossible, but without belief, it's infinitely more difficult. And if *you* don't believe in it, why should anyone else?

Apply this process not only to your ideas but to the ideas and opportunities other people bring to you. It's the best way to see if they're a fit for your personal journey of discovering the reality of success.

Accept the responsibility

With success—especially business and financial success—comes responsibility. As a successful person, you have the responsibility to use your money and other assets wisely, to be a good employer, to contribute to your community, to set a good example in all aspects of your life. You will be held to a higher standard. You'll come under a degree of scrutiny that unsuccessful people aren't under.

Are you prepared to accept the responsibility of success? If you're not, you may find that you're unable to hang onto it. If you are, you'll likely find yourself on the path to even greater success.

Les M. Goldberg

Homework

Write down your definition of success.

_____

_____

_____

_____

_____

_____

List the five people you spend most of your time with.
What characteristics do you have in common with them?

_____

_____

_____

_____

_____

_____

_____

_____

_____

_____

_____

_____

_____

_____

What is the biggest risk you've taken that worked out well?

_____

_____

_____

_____

_____

_____

What risk did you not take that you wish you had?

_____

_____

_____

_____

_____

_____

CHAPTER SEVEN

RELATIONSHIPS: THE PEOPLE IN YOUR WORLD

Relationship is the word we use to describe the way two or more concepts, objects, or people are connected. In this chapter, I'm going to focus on relationships between people. Strong, positive human relationships—both personal and professional—are an essential component of getting your stars aligned.

Most of us have what I call an inner circle, which is a group of a few close friends. These are the friends who really know you. They're the friends you would call if you were arrested and needed to be bailed out. Beyond that inner circle on a personal level are the people we know more casually, the people we see at social events, that we do various things with. On a business level are the people we work with, our customers, and our suppliers. Of course, it's common for crossovers to happen in business and personal relationships—a friend becomes a customer, a business associate becomes a friend.

Regardless of the type or degree of closeness, relationships are based on trust. When there's a lack of trust, or when the trust has been broken, the relationship is negatively affected. In business, the trust that's created with relationships is how things get done. People who trust you believe you when you make a commitment. They know you'll do what you say and say what you'll do.

The key to successful relationships is an understanding of their importance and a willingness to work on them.

Surround yourself with people who make you better

In Chapter 6, we talked about surrounding yourself with successful people. A key reason to do that is that those are the people who make you better, who challenge you to succeed, and who expand your horizons. We also talked about spending your time wisely. Relationships require time to build and maintain. If you're going to invest time in a relationship, make sure it's with quality people who make the world a better place and will help you be a better person.

Sometimes people will make excuses for having others in their business or social circle who don't meet the standards I'm advising you to set. Sometimes we compromise on those standards and hang out with people who aren't good for us but we understand their shortcomings, and we don't judge. We might feel like a better person because of their flaws, but they aren't actually helping us become better. That's not good for you or them. Set minimum standards for your friends and don't spend time with people who don't meet those standards. You only have so much time—don't invest it with people who are going to drain your energy and bring you down. Remember, you are a reflection of the people you spend time with, so spend your time with people who want to be better themselves and will help make you better.

No one is an expert at everything, so it's important to have people in your world who are smarter than you in various areas. And it's also important that you be that smarter person when it comes to your area of expertise. This keeps your relationships balanced so you can give as well as receive when it comes to counsel, support, and being a resource.

The people we are around will influence our behavior. One of the people who was a significant influence on me was my grandfather, Sam Tabachnick. He was an entrepreneur, and he loaned me the money to start LMG. When I was a kid, I played chess with him—he used the game to teach me about strategy. I'm sure I have a lot of his DNA, but even if we hadn't been related, he made a huge difference in my life.

When I start thinking about all the people who have inspired me, encouraged me, and in some way made me a better person, the list is almost endless. Throughout my life, I have made it a point to have positive relationships that are mutually beneficial on multiple levels. Most of my close friends are private people, so I'm not going to name them, but we provide support and advice, and we engage in friendly competition. There are times when our get-togethers are like an episode of *Shark Tank*, where one of us tosses out an idea and the others point out what's good and what's bad about it. We're good for each other. As much as I want to be around people who make me better, I also want to be a person who makes others better.

Look for ways to connect with people beyond your family and immediate social circle who will help you grow and become better, who will expand your horizons, who will challenge you to achieve.

I have been fortunate that, during my career, I have met hundreds of great achievers, over-achievers, successful entrepreneurs, and talented CEOs of huge corporations. Each one has inspired me and left me with at least a nugget that made me better.

One was Howard Lutnick, the chairman and CEO of Cantor Fitzgerald, a financial services firm headquartered in the World Trade Center. None of the firm's employees who were in the office on September 11, 2001, survived the attack; 658 of the company's 960 employees—including Lutnick's brother—died that day. Lutnick was dropping his son off at kindergarten, which caused him to be late to work and saved his life. Observers expected the devastated company to close, but Lutnick not only kept the firm alive, he has also become a well-known philanthropist. He used a terrible tragedy to create a new purpose for his business. The company had to recover and thrive to support the families of the people who died.

For the first 20-25 years of my career, I heard great

leaders speak every week. I saw their presentations and often saw them rehearsing. I soaked up everything they shared. George W. Bush (former President of the United States), Bill Gates (founder of Microsoft Corporation), Mikhail Gorbachev (president of the former Soviet Union), Al Gore (former Vice President of the United States), Steve Irwin (the Crocodile Hunter), Oliver North (combat-decorated U.S. Marine, bestselling author) and more all set a course for greatness in the world and I was fortunate enough to see them in person. Of course, that's the nature of my business, and not everyone will have that opportunity during their day-to-day work, but that doesn't mean you can't take advantage of their wisdom. Attend presentations,

> As much as I want to be around people who make me better, I also want to be a person who makes others better.

read books (like this one), listen to podcasts, watch You-Tube videos—identify the people you admire and soak up their message.

You want to be around people who influence you to function at your highest and best consistently. When you're down, you need people who can bring you back up and inspire you. Get people like that in your inner circle.

The other side of surrounding yourself with people who make you better is to avoid toxic people. You must learn to recognize when relationships are unhealthy and take steps to deal with it. You've got to either get off the bus and end the relationship or figure out what you need to do to make the relationship healthy. Don't let that toxicity impact your world.

You choose not to let someone else bring you down and make you unhappy. You can't control other people, but you can control how you react to them. Everyone has a choice every day to be happy.

I don't mean to sound callous, but it's no different than ridding your house of bugs. If there were a bug crawling in your house, you'd stomp on it or you'd kill it with pesticide, and get rid of it. You need to do the same thing with people who don't bring you happiness, who don't bring you up, who don't add anything to your life. You need to get them out of your life. Make a conscious decision that you're not going to invest your time with those people because it's not in your best interest and it's not bringing you happiness.

I understand that you may have a family member or a long-time friend who is going through a rough time and you want to help. That's fine. Help them to whatever extent you can. But in the process, protect yourself. Don't let them drag you down.

Who do you admire?

Who inspires you and why? You should know of at least five people who are inspirational to you in some form and be able to articulate who and why. These don't have to be people who you personally know or even who are currently living—although it's great if they are. They could be great business, spiritual, or even political leaders.

What did they accomplish? How did they do it? Why do you admire them?

I admire people who win against the odds, who overcome incredible obstacles, who can perform at the highest level in the toughest times. I admire people who take risks, knowing they're going to have either a great reward or a miserable failure. I admire people who have made this world a better place. My list of people I admire includes Nelson Mandela, Golda Meir, Martin Luther King, Jr., Henry Ford, Steve Jobs, Bill Gates, Warren Buffett, Walt Disney—I could go on. None of these people were perfect. They had flaws, and they made mistakes. Whether you agree or disagree with their personal or political philosophies is not the point. They left a legacy; they changed how we live our lives.

Having people in your life that inspire you to do great things is like putting a fuel additive in your car to make it run better. Why just putter along when you can soar?

Understand people so you can motivate them

We talked about the importance of motivation in Chapter 2. When your stars are aligned, you will be able to motivate yourself and others as well. But you can't motivate people you don't understand. That's why you need to know what makes the people in your world tick.

As an entrepreneur, one of my most important responsibilities is motivating my people. Business leaders have been perpetually challenged by how to figure out what it takes to motivate employees. The perennial question we ask ourselves is: What can I say or do to get you to perform at the highest possible level?

Over the years, I've come up with some effective answers and made a lot of mistakes. One of the key things I've learned is that people want to be on a winning team.

If they're playing sports, they want to play on a winning team. If they're working, they want to work for a winning company. They don't want to be part of a losing organization. I've been fortunate to have created a winning business staffed by a winning team. I've built a company that has shown strong growth and has an excellent reputation in our industry. That makes it easier to find the best people and the best people are easier to motivate.

Another key thing I've learned is that people want to be appreciated. In the workplace, people are often more motivated by having their hard work and effort acknowledged than they are by financial compensation. Of course, you can pay them more money, but money alone won't keep people performing at their best. Sometimes a simple, one-on-one compliment

Motivation is not a "one size fits all" thing. You have many different motivational avenues to take.

will do the job. Other times, more public praise is needed. In general, people need to know that others see and appreciate their hard work and effort. It's frustrating and disincentivizing to work really hard to accomplish something and not have it be recognized.

I think the best compliment is when you say good things about someone to other people. Of course, you want to make sure the subject of your praise knows about it. There are a lot of ways you can do this in a company, from programs like employee of the month to praising someone in public, such as when you introduce them (such as, "This is Mike. He's a topnotch IT guy and does a great job keeping our systems up and running."). Beyond motivating your employees with public praise, you can do the same with your suppliers and other colleagues. Leave online reviews, provide testimonials, give recommendations.

Be strategic and intentional in how you praise and never miss an opportunity to express genuine admiration and appreciation for people. Always praise in public and reprimand in private.

Another motivation strategy that can be extremely effective is to motivate people in advance. Show your gratitude by thanking them ahead of time for all the hard work you know they're going to do, for all the hard work it's going to take to accomplish a job. Let them know that you realize they're climbing a mountain but you know they can do it and you're confident the results will be amazing when they're done.

Something I used to do when I was working shows (and our team leaders do it now) is to go around before the show starts and give a passionate speech to the crew, saying something like this, "I want to thank you in advance. I know everybody's head is in the game, you've all worked hard to get ready, and you're all going to do a great job. So thank you—I know you're going to be great." It not only gives the crew confidence, it also sets the bar high. Nobody wants to be the one who wasn't great after they were told they were going to be great.

Understanding people and what motivates people is super important to getting your stars aligned. Some people are motivated by money; others are motivated by acknowledgment. Some people are motivated by public praise; others don't need it or even want it. Some people are motivated by knowing they're doing good for others.

Some people need to think that whatever you want them to do is their idea. You need to get their input before you can get their buy-in. Some people are happy to stay under the radar; for them, just knowing how they make a difference in the world or even in your company is enough.

The issue of motivation is closely related to emotional intelligence, which is defined as the capacity to be aware of, control, and express one's emotions, and to handle interpersonal relationships judiciously and empathetically.

Understanding your own emotional intelligence is the key to both personal and professional success. Understanding how you can apply it to others will help you motivate them because you'll know them well enough to identify what approach will produce the best outcome. We have a natural tendency to think that other people are motivated by the same things that motivate us, so we treat them as we want to be treated, but that doesn't work. I am motivated by the applause when the show was awesome, even though I'm not on the stage.

We have people on our team who love being the center of attention, who are fueled by admiration. But we also have introverts on our team who cringe at recognition, who find being in the spotlight demotivating, who just want to do their jobs and pack up and go home. It's the responsibility of their supervisors and managers to understand that, to get to know the people on their teams well enough so they can identify the approach that will produce the outcome we want. I have done this with our leadership team, and I expect every leader in our company to do it with the people they supervise. That's emotional intelligence in action.

Motivation is not a "one size fits all" thing. You have many different motivational avenues to take. Ultimately, if you understand the people you're surrounding yourself with and you take an analytical approach via emotional intelligence to deal with them in a way that will validate who they are and how they feel, you'll generally produce the best outcome. You'll help them become highly motivated.

I've discovered that some people have to be involved in formulating the plan to be motivated. I can't just tell them what my plan is; I get them involved so it becomes their plan, too. That creates buy-in. For others, I have to spend time describing the outcome, painting a picture of the destination so I can get them to realize how important the journey is. I get them on board by showing them where we're going. That helps to get everybody moving in the same direction. And then there are times when I motivate by stressing the consequences of failure and setting the expectation that failure is not an option. We have to succeed. We don't want our competitors to win. What do we have to do to be the winner? The key is to recognize that every person is unique and it is your responsibility as the leader to figure out what will motivate the various people on your team.

I've always found that the easiest way to make myself feel good is to make someone else feel good. With our employees, I do that by letting them know they're appreciated and expressing my gratitude for their contribution. It just takes a few seconds and a little effort to let someone who is working hard on your behalf know that you appreciate it, but the impact it has on them is tremendous. The key is to be sincere and selective. A specific, genuine compliment has great value, but if you go around all the time telling people how wonderful they are, your compliments lose their value.

Your biggest challenges in the area of motivation will come from negative people. As a general rule, I avoid dealing with them. It's hard to motivate them, and they bring me down. I don't want them in my world.

But people who are either neutral or positive—these are people I can work with, people I can motivate through using emotional intelligence techniques. I can convince them that together we can move mountains. They'll buy into my dream and make it their own. They know we're all in the same boat and we're rowing together.

I think there's a direct connection between happiness and motivation. Happiness is a byproduct of the process of fulfilling your purpose and realizing your dreams. Motivated people are happy. Unmotivated people are unhappy. I like being around happy people.

> *The easiest way to make myself feel good is to make someone else feel good.*

Understand your motivations

As important as it is to know what motivates others, it's even more important to be clear about what motivates you. With some introspection, you can figure that out. This will give you the insight and knowledge you need to create an environment where your stars can align.

Think of the times when you felt highly motivated. What was happening? What were you feeling? Now think of the times when you felt demotivated and demoralized and ask yourself the same questions. Write your answers down.

Pay attention to your feelings and what caused them. If you have a good day, figure out why it was good. Do the same thing if you have a bad day. Don't look at the external factors over which you have no control. Look at your attitude, your feelings, how you responded to situations.

For example, maybe you worked hard on a project but your efforts didn't have any impact on the final outcome, and that made you feel depressed. Or you worked hard and your contribution had a significant and positive impact on the final outcome. From that, you could say that you are motivated by feeling that what you contribute is making a difference.

Another example could be that you're assigned a task and given complete freedom to accomplish the desired result. That allows you to exercise your creativity and makes you feel valued and trusted. Or you were given a task accompanied by a lot of restrictive requirements that stifled your creativity and made you feel that you weren't being trusted to get the job done on your own. Either of these scenarios tells you that you are motivated by having a sense of freedom and autonomy in your work and by feeling valued and trusted.

Once you become aware of your feelings and what caused them, you'll be able to understand and prioritize your motivations. With that knowledge, you can develop a plan to make changes in your work situation so you stay motivated and satisfied. You might be motivated by being competitive and winning, or taking on seemingly impossible challenges, by learning new skills, or by having variety in your work. Or you might be motivated by working alone rather than with a team, or by operating in a low-risk environment where you don't have to take a lot of chances or make decisions. Motivations are not right or wrong, but you can't create the best environment for yourself if you don't clearly understand your motivations.

This applies to the people you work with as well. If you are a supervisor or leader, share this exercise with your team. Encourage them to share their motivations so that you can help them build an environment that works for them and the company.

Help others get their stars aligned

When you have the chance, help someone else who is trying to get their stars aligned. It's amazing how much that helps you. You'll feel good knowing you had a positive impact on someone else's life and you'll probably also learn something you can apply to your own life. It's one of the best win-wins you can do.

There are people who don't know what they want, who haven't figured out their passions. I call them lost in life. They're just puttering along without getting much accomplished. They go to work, they go home, they go through the motions, but they don't have a true *joie de vivre*, a real zest for life. Sometimes they don't even realize what they're missing. Sometimes they know they're missing something, but they don't know what it is or how to find it.

These people need an anchor. They need direction. And you could be the source that helps them find what they need. So when you have the opportunity to help someone who is lost, do it. Encourage them, be their mentor, help them find the path in life that will make them happy.

This doesn't have to be a huge, time-consuming undertaking. It could be a positive comment, a brief suggestion, or a half-hour conversation. For example, a couple of years after my book *Don't Take No for an Answer* was published, I got a message through LinkedIn from someone I didn't know. He wrote, "I read your book. I have a couple of questions. Is there any way you'd be up for a phone call?"

I had some time while I was driving, so I took his call. We talked for about twenty minutes. I answered his questions and gave him some advice. Later on, he thanked me profusely

If you're not paying attention, you're at a disadvantage.

and told me I had been extremely helpful. I don't know if I'll ever find out exactly how helpful or what happened, but I made a difference in his life and through that, made a difference for myself.

It's a big (or small) world

The world is both big and small—it depends on how you look at it. It's big in that it has so much to offer, so many different cultures. It's small in how connected we are, particularly when it comes to technology. Whichever outlook you prefer, I encourage you to broaden your horizons by seeing as much of the world as possible. And if you can't see it in person, study it in other ways.

I've been very fortunate to travel the world for both business and personal reasons. I've met people from all over the planet—people from different cultures, different societies, different socioeconomic statuses. That's given me a perspective I didn't have when I was young.

When I'm interacting with people, no matter where they're from, chances are I can relate to them to some degree because I've been so many places that we've probably got at least one experience in common. In my travels, I've done some things you might think are crazy and that most people wouldn't even consider.

Today, I can look back on all those experiences and see how they have made me a better person. I've climbed a pyramid in Egypt, been gorilla trekking in Uganda, seen what's left of the Berlin Wall, and dove the Great Barrier Reef. While doing those things (and more), I took the time to get to know the people, to understand their culture and lifestyle. My success has made it possible for me to do that—and doing that has afforded me even more success because of what I've learned.

Regardless of the size and scope of where you work, whether you're the owner or an employee, the fact is that there's no such thing as a strictly local business anymore. All business is global. We are connected around the world in ways we often don't think about and it's essential that we pay attention to what's going on. The stock market opens in China while we're all sleeping in the United States. By the time we wake up, a lot of things have happened. Even an independent neighborhood restaurant can be affected by something that happens on the other side of the world—a weather event could damage crops and you can't get the ingredients you need, a political event could raise or lower the price of energy. If you're not paying attention, you're at a disadvantage.

Dealing with betrayal

No matter how careful you are, you are going to encounter dishonest people, who will steal from you and betray you in other ways. That's just a fact of life. You can't avoid it, so be prepared to deal with it.

I'm a pretty good judge of character and most of the time I can sense whether a person is trustworthy and honest. Of course, when it comes to hiring, we also do thorough background checks. But sometimes a bad egg slips by. And sometimes people change. A person who was honest may decide to steal or a person who was loyal may do something disloyal.

> You are not responsible for the choices other people make or the actions they take.

How you respond to betrayal depends on the circumstances. As a general guideline, if it's something minor, talk it out and give the person a second chance. If it's major, you have to figure out if trust can be restored.

The toughest thing to deal with when someone betrays you is the emotional impact. Even if you are able to put on a strong front and not show your feelings, the reality is, betrayal hurts. It can cause you to doubt yourself. But know this: You are not responsible for the choices other people make or the actions they take. You may have to deal with the repercussions of what they do, but you are not responsible for it.

As with any life experience, when someone betrays your trust, do what you need to in order to resolve the situation, learn your lesson, and move on.

The choice in your relationships

The word karma means action. It's often used to mean the spiritual principle of cause and effect—essentially, what you do today has an impact on your future. I believe in karma. When people are good to others, good things come to them. When people are bad to others—maybe being cruel or unethical—that eventually comes back to them.

Do bad things happen to good people? Of course. But that's not the point I'm making here. My point is that over and over, in my business and personal life, I have seen the concept of what goes around, comes around play out. Every person you have a relationship with in your life, whether it's personal or business, will affect your life in some way. Whether it's a positive or negative impact is your choice.

Homework

Do something in the next 24 hours to make someone else happy without any expectation of a reward.

_____

_____

_____

_____

List the people in your circle who make you better.

_____

_____

_____

_____

_____

_____

_____

_____

List the people in your circle who drag you down. What are you going to do about those relationships?

_____

_____

_____

_____

_____

_____

_____

List five people who inspire you and why.

List your personal motivations (what motivates you?).

Where in the world would you like to go that you've never been? Commit to making that trip.

CHAPTER EIGHT

REPUTATION IS YOUR CURRENCY

Your reputation is your most valuable asset. A good reputation takes years to build. It's a reflection of the experience people have with you on all levels. If you don't have a good reputation, it's going to be extremely difficult for your stars to align.

Before we talk about why reputation is so important, let's understand what it is. Reputation is defined as the beliefs or opinions that are generally held about someone or something. Essentially reputation is about perception. It's about what other people are thinking and saying about you, and it may or may not be true or accurate.

Every one of us has a reputation. Because it's based on others' experience with us, our reputation may be different with different people or segments of our lives. You may, for example, have a reputation of being a rigid rule-follower with your colleagues at work but a soft touch with your family when it comes to your kids and their friends. Or you might have a professional reputation as a charming, outgoing person who will do whatever it takes to make a customer happy and a personal reputation as someone who is quiet but demanding of friends and family. Your reputation influences other people even before they meet you. It can make them decide to deal with you—or not. It can make them trust you easily or be extremely cautious.

Reputation is often confused with character. They're not the same. Reputation is what others think of you. Character is who you are. Abraham Lincoln said it this way: "Character is like a tree and reputation like a shadow. The shadow is what we think of it; the tree is the real thing." Of course, your character drives your conduct which creates your reputation, so the two go hand-in-hand. But even people of high integrity need to value and protect their reputations. Especially in this age of social media and instant communication, reputations can be damaged or even destroyed in a matter of hours or days. Sometimes it's justified, sometimes it isn't. But either way, it can take a long time to rebuild your reputation.

When you're highly visible, whether in your community, your industry, or in the public eye in general, your reputation is magnified. Most successful people find it difficult to fly under the radar, so they're going to be visible. And if they're smart, they will guard their reputation with everything they do.

So how do you protect your reputation? Most importantly, always do the right thing. Don't give people a reason to attack you. If you follow the Golden Rule of treating others as you want them to treat you, the chances your reputation will be tarnished are greatly reduced, and you'll be able to sleep at night. But that's not enough. It's possible these days for people to say things about you that are untrue and those things can spread around the world with amazing speed. Sadly, the negative will get more visibility than the positive. You'll find it hard to defend yourself.

A few years ago, a disgruntled former employee decided to create a fake Twitter account using my name. He started posting things that made me look bad— ugly, negative things that I don't feel and would

When you make a mistake, own up to it. Apologize and do what you can to make it right.

never say. Fortunately, my assistant spotted it shortly after the account went live, but it took a lot of time, determination, and effort to resolve the situation. Eventually, I was able to get Twitter to remove the fake account, and the police were able to identify the person behind it. He was arrested and reached a plea agreement with the prosecutor on several criminal charges.

I could have let it go once the fake account was taken down—which in itself wasn't easy because social media platforms are measured and valued by the number of accounts and the traffic they have, so they're not particularly motivated to close accounts. But the prosecutor encouraged me to follow through with the criminal side not only for myself but to establish case law that could be used to help protect other victims in the future.

The lesson for you is this: Monitor the internet, social

media, review sites, and similar places for what people are saying about you and your company. If someone has a legitimate complaint, address it immediately. When you make a mistake, own up to it. Apologize and do what you can to make it right. If you see something negative that's unfounded, promptly implement a response strategy. Of course, that strategy will vary depending on what's happening. If this is not your area of expertise, hire professional help. It's worth the investment.

No such thing as privacy

We have very little privacy anymore. While technology such as public databases and even private systems that share information is responsible for a large part of our decreased privacy, we bring a lot of it on ourselves. The most visible way we do that is on social media. I recognize that social media has a place in our world and it isn't going away. But keep in mind that what you share on social media is going to be out there forever. It's like getting a tattoo—it's permanent. The picture you posted or the comment you made might have seemed like a good idea at the time, but now you wish you hadn't done it—and it's too late to take it back.

Don't think something you share online is private just because you limited it to your friends. It can spread. Every day we see things in the news about someone's career being ruined by something they posted on social media years ago. Many companies make social media reviews a routine part of pre-employment background checks, so be super cautious about what you share on social media. Better to not share than to have something come back and bite you in a few years.

Another privacy issue to keep in mind is what you write in emails. Remember that everything you put in an email is subject to possible reproduction and distribution by others—and simply marking it "confidential" doesn't mean it will be kept confidential. The same thing applies to text messages and all other forms of electronic communication. Certainly, when you're running a business, you need to communicate confidential information to your team electronically, and you have to trust them. But you also need to remember that it's always possible that someone outside your company will see what you've written. Be sure it won't embarrass you or, worse, create some sort of legal exposure.

How big is your ego?

Ego is the Latin word for "I." As a psychoanalytical term, it has a complex meaning. But for general purposes, most of us use ego when we're talking about a person's sense of self-worth and self-esteem.

Everyone has an ego. It doesn't matter whether it's a big ego (often seen as conceit) or a little ego (modest and possibly insecure). Our egos drive many of our decisions. For example, if you bought a luxury home, did you do it for your own enjoyment or because you want others to know you have money and can afford it?

Successful people have to work to keep their egos in check—and they often fail. They might need to feel validated, so they find it necessary to brag to the world about how awesome and wonderful they are. That doesn't impress me. I'm far more impressed by people who are humble, who have accomplished a lot but don't feel the need to show off.

It's important to have a healthy ego, a positive sense of self-worth and confidence in your abilities. But when ego becomes exaggerated, it's often offensive. I know this from personal experience—there are times that I have to work to keep myself in check because my ego can get out of control.

Some signs of an oversized ego include:

Always having to be right and never admitting mistakes.

Never being satisfied and always wanting more.

Constantly engaging in one-upmanship.

Always having to win.

Requiring constant attention.

Talking excessively, using the word "I" in almost every sentence, interrupting frequently, not listening to others.

Lacking empathy.

Needing to be in a position of power.

Taking credit for the success of others, not giving others deserved credit.

Extremely opinionated.

Lacking and/or failing to express gratitude.

Do a periodic self-check for these characteristics. Be honest with yourself. If you see any of these traits in your behavior, take steps to deal with them before they knock your stars out of alignment.

It's all about integrity

When people start bragging about how much integrity they have, I'm suspicious. You shouldn't have to tell people that you're ethical. Having said that, let's talk about integrity and principles.

There is an unbreakable connection between integrity and happiness. If you don't have integrity, I don't think it's possible to be truly happy. In the same way, lies and misery go together.

I have strong principles, and I believe that's been a big reason behind my success. Though it hasn't happened often, there have been times when those princi-

There is an unbreakable connection between integrity and happiness.

ples cost me money because I won't do things that violate them, even if those things are lucrative. I believe you live and die with your principles. If you're principle-focused, principle-centered, and principle-driven in every aspect of your life, it's far easier to bring your stars into alignment than if you're not.

Having principles is a cornerstone of being successful. It's a key way your character manifests. If your character is built around doing the right thing, treating people the right way, treating people like you want to be treated, you have strong principles.

You can't separate who you are in business from who you are in your personal life. It doesn't matter how good you are at home if you cheat people at work. The same thing applies in reverse. Weak or strong, low or high, your principles are your principles. They're the core of who you are.

I don't want people in my world who lack principles, who lack integrity. I won't do business with them, and I won't socialize with them. The old saying of "burn me once, shame on you; burn me twice, shame on me" is a great policy. You only have to touch a hot stove once to know that it's hot. When someone shows you that they can't be trusted, believe them and get them out of your life.

If you've ever taken a sales training course, you've probably heard that people buy from people they know, like, and trust. Work to be that person in your relationships—especially when it comes to trust. Do what you promise. Don't promise something you can't or won't do. Words are cheap, but your actions are what count because they demonstrate your principles. No matter how rich or educated you become, no matter how cool or smart you think you are, what you do tells all.

We are imperfect people living in an imperfect world. You can have the highest of standards and still occasionally fail. If you do something wrong, accept responsibility and make it right. That's integrity. People with integrity are the kind of people I want to do business with and you should, too. Those are the people who are able to get their stars aligned so good things happen.

Homework

Describe your business reputation.

_____

_____

_____

_____

Describe your personal reputation.

_____

_____

_____

_____

What is your plan to protect your reputation?

_____

_____

_____

_____

_____

_____

_____

_____

_____

_____

How do you demonstrate your integrity?

_____
_____
_____
_____
_____
_____
_____
_____
_____
_____
_____
_____
_____
_____

CHAPTER NINE

BE YOUR BEST

When it comes to what you expect from yourself, set the bar high. Don't settle for just getting by—you owe it to yourself to always be the best you can be. Don't be average, be exceptional. Something I say all the time is that average is unacceptable. Set the bar high— the bar for yourself personally and professionally, for your company, for any situation in which you can control the outcome.

The concept of being your best is about putting 100 percent of your effort behind whatever you're doing. Not 80 percent, not 50 percent. It's about commitment. Are you completely committed? Are you completely all in? Because if you're not all in, it's hard to be super successful. The commitment to being your best makes it easier to get to and stay at that exceptional level. Will you occasionally slip? Of course. But because you spend most of your time functioning at best, it's easier to get back there when you fall.

It's easy to say "be your best," but how do you do it? What can you do to be your best consistently? I don't have all the answers, but I'm going to share what I do know in this chapter. Some of the sections are extremely short; that's on purpose because they are tactics that others have written volumes about. Use this as a guide to identify the subjects you need to know more about and do your homework.

Do the right thing

Always do the right thing, even when it's difficult. Sometimes doing the right thing is easy, but many times, it's hard. Doing the right thing can mean making difficult choices, having unpleasant confrontations, or holding others accountable. The world is full of temptations. The news is full of stories of people who seem to have it all—wealth, professional success, family—and yet they make poor choices that end up costing them far more than they would have gained.

In Chapter 8, we talked about integrity. Doing the right thing because it's the right thing is the essential definition of integrity. When you do the right thing, you'll always be able to sleep at night and look at yourself in the mirror in the morning.

Know your goals

In Chapter 2, we talked about the importance of setting goals. Goals are essential to being your best. And stretch goals—the goals that force you to reach—give you the additional motivation you need to excel.

Do an annual review of your goals and the progress you're making toward them. Pick a date that works for you. Some people like to do this in December so they're ready for the new year. Others do it in January. Still others pick a different time of year such as their birthday or a meaningful anniversary. When you do it doesn't matter as long as you get it done.

If you've reached some of your goals, celebrate and set new ones. If your plan isn't working, figure out what you need to change. When you stay in touch with your goals, you stay motivated to achieve them.

Maintain a positive attitude

Being your best also means staying positive. A positive attitude is contagious—let the people around you catch it. Being positive gives you energy and helps you attract good people and good things. Being negative wastes energy. If you have a negative attitude, if you're filled with the venom of negativity, no matter how many good things are trying to come around you, they won't be able to happen.

Be thankful

You've probably heard this before: develop an attitude of gratitude. Be thankful for what you have, for what you can do, and for what others do for you.

We all know people who wake up in the morning and start complaining. If they can't find something real to complain about, they make something up. That's such a horrible, negative way to see life. Nobody wants to be around complainers—so don't be one.

If you wake up and have your faculties about you, if you're able to get up and go to school or work or whatever you have to do, if you have a few friends you know you can count on, you have so many reasons to be thankful. Good things don't have to be big or complicated. Sometimes good things are as simple as a kind word or gesture. And when you are on the receiving end of something good, remember to express your thanks to the source. It's amazing how quickly being consciously grateful can boost your energy and help align your stars.

Give

Anne Frank wrote, "No one has ever become poor by giving." I'll take that a step further and say that giving makes you rich—rich in the ways that truly matter.

The more you have, the greater your responsibility to give back. For many people, this understanding comes to us as we mature. I see it in many of my friends who are successful and financially well-off—they're discovering causes that are near and dear to their hearts, and they are giving generously to those causes. But you don't have to wait until you have a lot of money to give. You can do it now.

Support your community. Do it personally as well as through your business. Choose a charity that matters to you and support it both financially and through your actions.

In addition to making cash and in-kind contributions to various charities, I like to give away copies of my book, *Don't Take No for an Answer*. Often people I give it to will ask me to sign it. I tell them I'm happy to—if they donate the retail price of the book to my favorite charity, St. Jude Children's Research Hospital. I've never had anyone refuse; they almost always hand me more cash than what they would have paid if they'd bought the book in a store. I make sure the money is forwarded to St. Jude's with an additional contribution from me. Everybody wins.

The benefits of giving aren't limited to supporting charities. Giving takes so many forms other than simply writing a check. Yes, giving money is important and if you've got it, you should give at least some of it away. Organizations need cash to operate. But the gift

You don't have to wait until you have a lot of money to give. You can do it now.

of yourself, of your passion and commitment, is something you'll never be able to put a price tag on. And the more you do it, the better person you'll become.

Help others achieve success

Don't stay so focused on your own goals that you don't take the time to give others a hand up on their journey. You can't put a price tag on the feeling of satisfaction you'll get from doing that.

I'm passionate about entrepreneurship, and I believe that, as a successful entrepreneur, I have a responsibility to help the next generation of entrepreneurs. It's my job to inspire them, and they inspire me. I'm inspired by their desire to want to create and do things, to be successful. And it's my responsibility to do anything I can to encourage them, to be a positive role model for them, to foster their belief that anything is possible—because it is! I do a variety of things to meet that responsibility, including teaching classes and speaking on entrepreneur-ship at colleges and other events, as well as working with young entrepreneurs one-on-one to advise and mentor them.

Back before I officially launched LMG, I met a guy who had a mobile DJ business. I was still in high school and building my AV company. I helped him get some equipment he needed, and we became friends. Eventually, I convinced him to open his own nightclub instead of working gigs at other locations; today, he owns successful clubs in eight cities. Without my initial encouragement, he might not have opened that first small club that grew into a multimillion-dollar business.

Not all of my efforts to help others succeed are so dramatic. Sometimes it's a simple matter of making sure an employee has the resources necessary to achieve and grow. Sometimes it's making referrals so that suppliers I use and trust can grow their businesses. I've supported and encouraged employees who have decided they wanted to go out on their own and start their own companies—companies that eventually became our customers. Help-ing others succeed doesn't always have a direct impact on my financial bottom line, but the impact on my sense of personal satisfaction and happiness is priceless.

Make the world better

Do something every day, however small, to make the world a better place. This is an imperfect world, but that's no reason not to try to improve it. From things as small as holding a door or helping someone carry a load of pack-ages to making a substantial charitable contribution, you have the ability to make a difference, to leave a legacy of some sort. Make your legacy a good one.

Don't worry

Too many people waste too much energy worrying. Worry is totally non-productive and can be destructive. Things are either in your control or they're not. If it's in your control, do everything you can to position yourself to be a winner. If it's not in your control, there's nothing you can do. In either case, worrying won't help, so don't do it. Instead, take the energy you would waste on worrying and use it to build contingency plans and take other steps to reduce the chances something bad will happen. That will let you worry less and focus more on what you want to accomplish.

Love what you do

There's a proverb that says if you love what you do, you don't count the hours. That's true. There's also a proverb that says if you love what you do, you'll never work a day in your life. That one isn't true. You'll work, but you won't count the hours. The time will fly by. If you find yourself in a job that you hate, counting the hours, you need to make a change.

The reality is that we're not going to passionately love every single thing we have to do to get through each day. I don't love reading contracts but I do it because it's part of my responsibility as the CEO and president of my company—and I love being the CEO and president of my company. I don't love dealing with situations where someone has dropped the ball and there's a problem that needs

133

to be fixed or when I have to fulfill obligations that are frustrating and unpleasant, but I do those things happily because I love what I do.

When the hours fly by, when you look forward to each new day, when you're excited even when you're putting out fires—that's when you love what you do.

Make each day a new beginning

Wake up each morning with the attitude that it's a new day and it's going to be great. Whatever happened yesterday is in the past—let it go. How you start the day is a major impact on how you'll finish it, so decide from the minute you open your eyes what kind of a day you're going to have. Know what your goals for the day are and have a plan to achieve them. Be confident and ready for success.

Practice continual improvement

Your best today is far better than it was a few years ago and not as good as it will be in the future. Constantly challenge yourself to improve in every aspect of your life. Get out of your comfort zone. Don't dwell on your mistakes; acknowledge them and use them to learn and grow. Practice your skills, get a coach, read books, take classes—do whatever it takes so that you will wake up every morning better and wiser than you were the day before and thankful for it.

Write it down

Make writing things down a habit. We've all got so much to keep track of that it's impossible to keep it all in our heads. But we've all got smartphones, so making notes is easier than ever. I've had so many great ideas that would have been lost had I not immediately put them into my phone. In fact, I created the initial outline of this book on my phone.

Writing things down not only helps you remember things, whether it's appointments, *Make your legacy* tasks, or ideas, it helps you clarify *a good one.* them. When you write things down, it's easier to see what's working, what isn't, what's missing, what needs to be tossed. Making notes of meetings, conversations, and your thoughts also creates a record if you ever need it.

Figure out an organizational system for writing things down that works for you and use it.

Do it 100 percent

I've said this before, but I can't stress it enough: Don't do things halfway. Be 100 percent all in, whatever you're doing.

When I wake up in the morning, my mind is racing before I get out of bed. There is so much going on in my world and I'm so juiced about it that it's hard for me to sleep. I can't wait for the sun to come up so I can tackle what's on my agenda for the day. I'm 100 percent all in, whatever I'm doing. That's the level of enthusiasm and commitment you need, too.

See problems as opportunities

Adversity comes in so many different forms. It can be something as minor as car trouble or as major as a key person in your organization leaving abruptly. It could be health issues, equipment failures, natural and manmade disasters, even accidents and mistakes.

Obstacles are a part of life. You can either overcome them or let them overcome you. Problems don't just go away; you need to address them as soon as you become aware of them. When you have a problem, immediately invest time and energy to find a viable solution. If you don't, it will only become a bigger problem. That's why successful people are effective problem-solvers.

When you let yourself be overwhelmed by a bad situation, you may not be able to think clearly or take the necessary steps to deal with it. So don't allow life's un-avoidable adversities to be bigger and stronger than you are. Don't let them drain your energy or stop you from reaching your goals. It's natural to fear adversity until you change your disposition and develop the habit of see-ing opportunities instead of problems.

Learn from your mistakes

If you don't learn from your mistakes, you'll repeat them. It's a simple concept. And while it may be obvious, how often do we fail to do this?

If you make a mistake and learn what not to do again, you become a better person.

My mistakes have taught me more lessons than anything else. They've taught me what not to do, how to avoid problems, what to do better next time.

Bad decisions come with a cost, and that cost is one way to put a value on your mistakes. I use that concept of figuring out what a mistake cost us—not just the actual dollars but the damage in customer relations and our rep-utation—to educate our team so we know what to do the next time we're in that situation. Everybody says they try to avoid mistakes; we are proactive about doing everything we possibly can to prevent them.

Part of the process of learning from mistakes is taking responsibility for them and doing what you can to make things right. Every time you're in a difficult situation where you have to find a way out, a solution, you grow a little bit. I'm not suggesting that you break out the champagne when you make a mistake, but if you make a mistake and learn what not to do again, you become a better person.

Celebrate your successes

As important as it is to learn from your mistakes, don't just focus on failures and what you can learn from them. Take the time to celebrate when things go right.

As learning experiences, we tend to treat successes differently than failures. When we get the results we want, we often don't take the time to reflect on how we did everything right. That's understandable because when you're running a business, whether you're an owner or manager, it's hard to stop and enjoy your successes; there's always something else to do, another project, another deal, another challenge. The wheels keep turning. The accolades for a success don't seem to last as long as the pain of a failure. The pain of failure seems to last forever. But when we do it right, we often just say "good job" and move on. That's not good. It's important to reflect, to enjoy, to savor your successes. Also, from a practical view, there's value in taking the time to look at what you do right so you can do it again. In an organization, the wins can be used as super rocket fuel to keep people motivated.

Don't wait until the end of a journey to celebrate. Mark the milestones along the way. Let's say you're working on a big project and there are ten key steps or ten places where you get to say, "Okay, that's done. We can move to the next phase." You get to step four and it was a huge challenge, it had more hurdles than you expected. Before you go on to number five, celebrate completing number four. You worked hard, you overcame obstacles, and you're closer to your goal. Take the time to savor that.

Much of our self-worth as human beings is driven through the sense of accomplishment. It's a universal feeling, whether you bake a delicious cake, catch a big fish, score well in a sport, or close a big deal. It doesn't matter what milestone you achieve, you owe it to yourself to savor the sense of accomplishment.

There will be times when, no matter how hard you try, you'll fail. So celebrate your wins.

Homework

What subjects in this chapter most resonated with you and why?

_____

_____

_____

_____

_____

_____

_____

_____

_____

Which ones do you need to learn more about? How are you going to do that?

_____

_____

_____

_____

_____

_____

_____

_____

_____

_____

What charity either do you or will you support? What will
you give in terms of action and financial contributions?

_____

_____

_____

_____

_____

Think of a problem that you were able to turn into an opportunity. How can you duplicate that process?

_____

_____

_____

_____

_____

_____

_____

What are you going to do to celebrate your next win?

_____

_____

_____

CHAPTER TEN

AN AMAZING JOURNEY

My life has been an amazing journey, and I want yours to be one, too.

My journey has been one of continuous learning and that's one of my biggest joys. I learned from the people I worked for before I started my own business. I've learned and continue to learn from the people I work with now— my company's employees, customers, suppliers. And I've learned from my family and friends.

Even though it wasn't always intentional, the people in my life have greatly enriched my knowledge and helped me become a wiser person. Do I know everything? Of course not. But I know a lot and I'm thankful every time I have an opportunity to share, to provide counsel to someone.

My office is a testament to my attitude toward life and business. It's not cluttered, but the décor includes symbols of things that are important to me and keep me motivated. For example, I keep a rainstick in my office. A rainstick is a hollow tube partially filled with pebbles or beans that make a noise that sounds like rain. It reminds me that, as the owner of a company, I need to make it rain. I need to pursue opportunities. Even though I have a sales and marketing team, I have the ultimate responsibility for rainmaking. That's something all successful entrepreneurs understand. They know they have to make it rain, they have to bring business in, they have to conquer the world.

I also have models of the airplanes I have owned. I'm proud of those airplanes. Before I got the first one, I didn't think I could afford it. Then I realized I couldn't afford not to have it. It's a tremendous productivity tool. Yes, it's expensive to own and operate a plane. I've had to work hard to make money to pay for the planes I've owned. But in addition to making me more efficient, they're a symbol of success, so I keep the models in my office where I can see them every day. They remind me to celebrate the wins and help fuel my drive.

Winning is important to me, so I have several other items in my office that represent winning, like a Willie Wonka golden ticket. I have a large, beautiful picture of Las Vegas—not only because we do a lot of business there (although we do), but because Vegas represents taking risks and winning. Don't misunderstand—casino gambling is only a good business strategy if you own the casino. But the concept that winning requires a degree of risk drives most of my decision-making.

But it's not all business. A full wall of family pictures reminds me of what's really important in my life. It helps me maintain perspective.

What are you most proud of?

We talked about pride in Chapter 5 as one of the characteristics successful people share. When I want to get to know someone better, I ask them what they're most proud of. In addition to being a great job interview question, it's a way to get people to open up about themselves in other situations. It's a deep question, and their answers will tell you a lot.

Some people immediately gravitate to talking about their family and kids. Other people will gravitate to their professional life and talk about their business achievements. Or they might be particularly proud of earning an advanced degree in their field.

> *What are you most proud of? Reflect on that in a positive way. Remind yourself of it regularly.*

Here's how I answer that question: I'm most proud of the fact that at a young age, I figured out what I wanted to do and I was able to pursue my dream and go all in and have a relatively high level of success. I was able to maintain a family life balance and prioritize my kids' events so my work life didn't usurp my family life. To be able to do both of those—business and family—and have good outcomes on both sides, is what I'm most proud of.

Of course, I've had time to think about it and to write out my answer. A lot of times, I hit people with that question with no warning and they don't know what to say. So I'm encouraging you to think about it now—what are you most proud of? Reflect on that in a positive way. Remind yourself of it regularly.

As I look back on my life, I know that I've been

fortunate, that a lot of things happened to me because I was in the right place at the right time and my stars fell into alignment. But it wasn't an accident for me, and it won't be for you. I worked hard to create an environment where positive things could happen. I paid attention and was prepared to take advantage of opportunities when they occurred. I never stopped learning and trying to be better.

In Chapter 1, I told you that I feel like I won the lottery a long time ago and just didn't realize it at the time. But I know it now. And I've come to understand that one of my life's purposes is to help others feel that way. I know what I did to get my stars aligned and I've shared that with you in this book so you can do it, too.

Getting your stars aligned is not a mystery. There's no secret. It's a simple matter of self-awareness and hard work.

Thank you for allowing me to be a part of your journey.

Homework

Make a list of what you are most proud of.

_____

_____

_____

_____

_____

_____

_____

_____

_____

_____

Now that you've finished this book, decide what you're going to do next. Write it down.

_____

_____

_____

_____

_____

_____

_____

_____

_____

Live your dreams.

ACKNOWLEDGMENTS

To list all the people who have in some way contributed to this book would be a book itself—and an impossible task. But I want to acknowledge all the hard-working, dedicated team members who have worked at any of my ETP companies from the very beginning to now and have helped us be successful.

The guiding counsel of the ETP leadership team is reflected not only in our company's success but in the pages of this book. As they have helped the ETP companies grow, they have helped me grow.

For her endless patience and ability to put up with me, I thank my trusted assistant, Stacy Teal.

From concept to published book, Jacquelyn Lynn played a vital role in helping me articulate my message by providing essential writing, editorial, and design skills.

Dave John and Robyn Baker provided invaluable input by reading the manuscript before it was final and offering excellent suggestions.

Finally, I want to acknowledge you, the reader, for without you, there would be no reason for this book. I hope you are better for having read it.

Les M. Goldberg

ABOUT LES. M GOLDBERG

Les M. Goldberg's professional titles include founder, chief executive officer, and president, but a more accurate description is that he is the driving force behind one of the entertainment technology services industry's leading players.

He started LMG in 1984 at the age of 17 with a $5,000 loan from his grandfather. LMG has grown from a small video equipment rental operation to a global leader in show technology, touring, and systems integration.

In 2014, Les created Entertainment Technology Partners (ETP), a parent company to a collection of exceptional brands in the industry. ETP's first acquisition was LMG. Under his guidance, the company has implemented a strategic acquisition plan that will support its brands as they take their performance to ever-higher levels.

Les is the author of *When All the Stars Align: Create a Life Where Great Things Happen* and *Don't Take No for An Answer: Anything is Possible.*

In addition to being an industry leader and active in the community, Les is a devoted family man. He makes his home in Orlando with his wife and their three children.

Connect with Les M. Goldberg

Visit Les's website, read his blog:
www.LesMGoldberg.com

Connect with Les on LinkedIn:
www.linkedin.com/in/lesmgoldberg

Follow Les on Twitter
www.twitter.com/LES_GOLDBERG

Les M. Goldberg

Don't Take No for an Answer

Anything is Possible

How one entrepreneur dreamed big and made it happen.

It's a success story that makes you want to stand up and cheer: Les M. Goldberg started his company at 17 as a way to make money doing something he loved while he was going to college. That small operation has grown into a multi-million-dollar entertainment technology industry leader.

In *Don't Take No for an Answer*, Les Goldberg uses wit and wisdom to tell the tale of his phenomenal success and share the techniques and tactics that have worked for him—and will work for you.

Available at your favorite online book retailer.

INVITE
LES M. GOLDBERG
TO SPEAK AT YOUR
NEXT EVENT

Beyond his passion for his own business, Les is passionate about entrepreneurship and enjoys sharing his expertise with a variety of audiences ranging from business students to corporate executives.

To invite him to speak at your next event, please contact: admin@lesgoldberg.com.

ENTERTAINMENT
TECHNOLOGY PARTNERS

Entertainment Technology Partners (ETP) is the parent company to a collection of exceptional brands in the live event and entertainment technology services industry. Our shared philosophy embraces a distinctive approach to quality, service, and support.

We are integrated industry leaders driven by client relationships and focused on the goal of building and growing business. We're relentlessly looking for new and innovative ways to do it, be it a new technology or a more efficient way to better serve our customers.

ETP provides the platform to facilitate growth through strategic alliances, expanded assets, value creation and geographic reach. Our markets include corporate events and conventions, concert tours, fixed installations, theater, television and film, and special events.

To learn more about ETP, please visit us online at ETP.net or email info@ETP.net.

Made in the USA
Middletown, DE
05 July 2019